JOHN
GREAT TO MEET A LIVING
legend.
All the best

David

RISK

and the

SMART
INVESTOR

USING THE
PRINCIPLES OF DE-RISKING
TO MAKE BETTER INVESTMENT AND
FINANCIAL DECISIONS

DAVID X MARTIN

New York Chicago San Francisco Lisbon London Madrid Mexico City
Milan New Delhi San Juan Seoul Singapore Sydney Toronto

The **McGraw·Hill** *Companies*

1 2 3 4 5 6 7 8 9 0   DOC/DOC   1 9 8 7 6 5 4 3 2 1 0

ISBN   978-0-07-174349-5
MHID   0-07-174349-9

This publication is designed to provide accurate and authoritative information in regard to the subject matter covered. It is sold with the understanding that neither the author nor the publisher is engaged in rendering legal, accounting, securities trading, or other professional services. If legal advice or other expert assistance is required, the services of a competent professional person should be sought.

>   —*From a Declaration of Principles Jointly Adopted by a Committee of the American Bar Association and a Committee of Publishers and Associations*

McGraw-Hill books are available at special quantity discounts to use as premiums and sales promotions or for use in corporate training programs. To contact a representative, please e-mail us at bulksales@mcgraw-hill.com.

This book is printed on acid-free paper.

CONTENTS

INTRODUCTION

"It is not necessary to change. Survival is not mandatory."
—W. Edward Deming

Whenever I hear someone say they see a light at the end of the tunnel, my first thought is that it might be the headlight of an oncoming train. In other words, I don't believe that just *any* light will necessarily show me the safest way through the darkness, any more than I believe that the darkness is something you have to *get through* in order to see the light. An overabundance of light, after all, can create a "blindness" as unnerving as the darkness itself; just ask anyone who looks up at the sun on a clear summer day. Furthermore, I strongly believe that the darkness of uncertainty can actually *create* the light of understanding, in the sense that learning to find your way in the dark can lead to new ways of thinking, force you to learn from your mistakes, and make you stronger and more resilient.

Whether or not we *gain* anything from moving through occasional periods of darkness, we must decide which path is most likely to lead us back to the light. Looked at in this way, a mineshaft, with many passageways to the surface, is a far more apt metaphor than a tunnel. One light, seen from afar, may lead you to stumble into an unseen chasm, while another might lead you safely to fresh air.

In other words, we cannot make decisions based solely on what we see, or what we *think* we know. In fact, our decisions are always based on *incomplete* information, and as a result we have to learn to manage the risks associated with a decision-making process that is by its nature imperfect.

In the financial world, for instance, we can never know exactly which way consumer sentiment will swing; what the monthly employment figures will be; how many homeowners will be able to pay their mortgages; or how high or low the demand will be for commodities, products, or services. And just as importantly, we can never know how the markets will respond to these and other unforeseen developments. And it is for that reason—because we can never know with *certainty* which way is best—that we need sound principles to help guide us through the darkness. These principles, of risk management and decision making, will require most of you to *change* the way you find your way through the inevitable periods of darkness, but as Deming notes, such a change is not necessary— that is, unless you wish to survive.

More than 30 years ago I was a student of archeology, and did my field work in the Middle East. The temperature extremes were surreal. When we worked out in the open air, we started around 5:00 a.m. and quit just before noon, when the sun was overhead and the heat made the job impossible. When we worked in caves— in the cold, wet, darkness, and covered from head to toe so we would not be bitten by ticks—we would walk back outside into the sunlight, and fully dressed were almost immediately at risk of heat exhaustion. It was painstaking work, hard on the eyes, the back, and the legs, especially when you consider that the tools we used were similar to those used by dentists—that is, small picks and brushes.

And once we had cleared a small area, we then poured the loose dirt through strainers to be sure we didn't miss anything. Mostly we found animal bones, shards from clay pots, and small rocks of no significance.

While we found no *things* of importance, we learned a great deal about earlier cultures, both in the field and the classroom. At our desks we studied the work of Kathleen Kenyon, whose stratigraphic excavation at Jericho had revealed 5,000-plus years of history, from straw huts to the City's fabled walls. The heart of Kenyon's discovery was the cycle of destruction and renewal that had occurred at the *same site.* Jericho had been occupied for millennia, and Kenyon's excavation catalogued not only the incremental advance of civilization, from flint knives to bronze spearheads, but the appearance, disappearance, and resurgence of basic principles of planning—of walls ringing the town, of town squares where inhabitants rubbed shoulders with one another, of granaries, wells, and homes. In other words, later civilizations built their structures directly on top of those that had come before them, following principles that had been discovered and then lost, a cycle that occurred over and over again throughout history.

One need only consider that Rome, home to more than a million persons at the time of Christ, had shrunk to a city of 50,000 as the Dark Ages began. Every period of renewed growth, however, was characterized by a return to certain fundamental principles of city planning, many of which transcended Roman culture. Climb the Eiffel Tower, for instance, and look down on the city that Napoleon built. Then climb the Washington monument, and you will see a similar design, given the French influence on that city's construction, though the two cultures varied greatly.

Better yet, look upon Pompeii, now dug free of the ashes of Vesuvius, and see a city that is remarkably like modern Italian towns. Although not rectilinear, due to its topography, it is laid out in a grid of sorts, and features a central forum, a stadium, a marketplace, a water tower, and public baths. The nobility built their houses at the edge of the town, and still farther away, one found the cemetery. The town, which may have had as many as 20,000 inhabitants by 79 A.D., at the time of the eruption, had been settled centuries earlier, and grew as a result of the fertile volcanic soil. The source of that fertility, however, also led to the town's destruction.

In other words, anything that comes into being and survives—whether cities, political authorities, cultures, corporations—is built upon fundamental, enduring principles, and whenever such entities fail they are eventually reborn following those same principles. Einstein, for instance, gazing in wonder at the orderly nature of the universe, was convinced that some higher power must have been behind it. We see evidence of that order all around us—in the steady change of the seasons and the action of the tides, in cataclysmic destruction and the renewal of life—and yet we often fail to consider this order, and its defining principles, when we "make" our own worlds. And this is true whether we speak of our personal world or our financial world. We are convinced that these times are different, that the old rules no longer apply. We are distracted by momentary gain, and bored with long-term plans. We know the value of hard work, and yet constantly seek to avoid it. And this approach cripples our ability to make sound decisions in all aspects of our lives.

Risk management, as it is practiced *today* in the financial world, is a mere child, born in response to the financial fraud of the late 1980s. But its principles are not new, and its most recent appearance is simply the latest sign that our economic framework, and to some extent even our entire culture, has lost its way. We build in the light of the day, and stumble and fall in the night, and in the process bring our own work down around us. And this is as true in the world of finance as it is in our personal lives, and one need look back only a year or two for compelling proof.

The Financial Crisis

In September, 2008, a financial whirlwind bore down on one of the most prominent companies on the American economic landscape— Lehman Brothers Holdings, Inc. The storm had been gathering strength since the spring of 2007, when the subprime mortgage industry began to collapse. Within a year, in March, 2008, it had reached hurricane force. By then, the Dow Jones Industrial Average had fallen 20 percent from its October, 2007 peak, the residential real estate market had suffered the largest drop in sales of existing homes in more than 25 years, and the Federal Reserve, by agreeing to put up as much as $30 billion to cover potential losses, had overseen the fire sale of Bear Stearns to JPMorgan Chase.

As a veteran of both the Latin American Debt Crisis in the 1980s and the Asian Financial Crisis in the late 1990s, I felt a familiar chill down my spine as the storm winds began to swirl around Lehman Brothers. Those earlier crises, however, despite wreaking significant damage in financial markets around the world, did not threaten the global financial system itself. In the fall of 2008, however, my colleagues and I watched with growing concern as the hurricane finally made landfall in New York City, the financial capital of the world.

As Chief Risk Officer of one of the world's leading investment firms I was no mere bystander; my company had dealt with Lehman Brothers for decades. So, while I supported the theory of moral hazard—that is, that only the possibility of failure prevents individuals and institutions from taking unreasonable risks—I was also aware of the well-established doctrine "too big to fail." In other words, when unforeseen economic forces threatened the stability of a large financial institution in the United States, the Federal Reserve and the U.S. Treasury could be trusted to step in and prevent disaster.

This trust was based on experience, not faith, and there were no shortage of examples. In 1980, soon after I began my career in the financial world, the U.S. government provided loan guarantees to prevent a bankruptcy filing by Chrysler Corporation. About a decade later, in 1989, Washington created the Resolution Trust Corporation in order to liquidate underperforming assets—most of them mortgage-related—of savings and loan associations. Then, as the twentieth century drew to a close, and a consortium of Wall Street giants including Goldman Sachs, AIG, and Berkshire Hathaway failed to save Long Term Capital Management, a highly leveraged hedge fund that blew up in 1998, the Federal Reserve Bank, fearing a crisis of confidence in the credit markets, organized a bailout supported by contributions from the industry's major players.*

In 2008, however, neither the U.S. government nor the major players on Wall Street stepped up to save Lehman Brothers, and in a certain sense the "death" of the firm is a textbook example of the

---

* Lehman Brothers was one of the firms involved. Bear Stearns was not.

"inevitable" happening so quickly that nothing could be done—nothing, that is, except trying to find the courage to face the end.

The failure of Lehman Brothers, and the economic chaos that resulted, drove home the point that our financial system is built on more than free market principles and regulatory compliance. It also depends on a certain level of trust. For that reason, when the industry as a whole lost confidence in Lehman Brothers something I call "entanglement risk" occurred. In short, the transactions of the major financial institutions were—and are—so intertwined that the loss of confidence in one firm, and the devaluation of its assets, led to something far more dangerous to the system than simple financial loss—it led to what can best be termed "financial gridlock."

In order to understand how that happened, it is necessary to consider five factors: classical economic theory, securitization, regulation, valuation, and politics.

Classical market theory is perhaps best exemplified by two fundamental principles, the roots of which can be traced to the physical sciences: First, if you know the starting point, speed, and direction of an object you can accurately predict its future location; and second, any object affected by external forces eventually reaches a new equilibrium. In other words, we can predict the point at which a ball, rolled at a certain speed, on a particular trajectory, over a defined surface, will come to rest. The problem with the classical, predictive model is that it does not account for unprecedented shocks—something the economy delivers with all too quickly forgotten frequency. And when these shocks occur, as they inevitably do, the ball not only shifts course, coming to rest in unanticipated locations—it occasionally *rolls right off the table*. In other words, the power to predict economic outcomes is utterly dependent on our ability to consider *all* possible influences and outcomes in advance. And of course by now we know this to be impossible, even with the lessons of the past few years to guide us. No one can ever know with certainty exactly where the ball will end up or when, or when it will begin to move again.

These principles also lurk behind the Efficient Market Hypothesis, which presumes that all investors are rational, that prices result from the judicious appraisal of information available to everyone, and further, that the prices of all assets are determined using the same method, independently of one another. While this hypothesis has been responsible for a great deal of valuable economic and financial research, even the casual reader will notice that this theoretical world bears little resemblance to the one in which we live.

Securitized assets, for example, are products designed with the above assumptions in mind. In short, securitization is the process by which cash-flow producing assets—for instance, mortgage payments, credit card payments, auto loan payments, etc.—are bundled into asset-backed securities. The streams of interest and principal payments on the individual loans, however, are not commingled— they are divided into tranches, or sections, each receiving a different credit rating depending on the creditworthiness of *that portion* of the underlying debt. The holders of the highest-rated, or senior tranches, are the first to receive payment. Those holding the lower-rated tranches receive payment in turn, and because of the risk inherent in that arrangement, are rewarded with a higher return. In this way, asset-backed securities spread risk very efficiently—at least in theory—as long as the underlying cash flow continues. When even a portion of that cash flow is interrupted, however, determining the value of the entire asset-backed security becomes problematic. Therefore, if asset-backed securities like these figured in your portfolio—or were held by the investment firm with which you did business—and like most investors, you did not understand their complexities, in 2007–2008 you quickly found yourself unable to de-risk your position. Knowing where you are, then, is the first principle of risk management. And if you are unable to calculate the value of your holdings, or to understand the risks associated with them, then you have ceded control to the markets, and any student of recent financial history knows where that leads.

Which brings us to valuation. Securitized assets are traded only in dealers' markets. In other words, there is no marketplace—like the New York Stock Exchange for equities—where willing buyers and sellers can depend on being able to transact business, and where a transparent, tradable price is always available. Instead, because dealers "make" the markets they can also close the doors—due to capital requirements, changes in investor sentiment, or loss aversion—and when that happens a verifiable "market" price no longer exists, *because there is no longer a market.* And if you're holding mortgage-backed securities (MBS) when this happens, you'll be one of the ones left standing up when the music stops—and the chance to de-risk your position will be long gone.

Regulation can further aggravate market conditions, and sure enough as economic conditions worsened in the fall of 2008, Financial Accounting Standards Board (FASB) regulation 157, issued two years earlier, put additional pressure on those institutions holding mortgage-backed securities. In essence, the regulation mandated the use of "observable prices"—that is, valuing assets at the price for which they could be sold today, not at which they were bought yesterday. But in the absence of a market—and by the fall of 2008 the trading of mortgage-backed securities and collateralized debt obligations (CDO), or bundled MBS, had come to a complete halt—the regulation caused assets to be significantly undervalued, almost without consideration for the cash flow upon which they were built. Ratings agencies played a part as well. Despite the collapse of the mortgage industry, which began with New Century's bankruptcy in the spring of 2007, and continued on through IndyMac's bankruptcy in the summer of 2008, Moody's steadfastly maintained its A1 rating of Freddie Mac's preferred stock until August, 2008, a month before Lehman Brothers collapsed. Had the ratings agencies issued *accurate* assessments of these asset-backed securities a year earlier, those ratings would have helped rein in increasingly dangerous behavior—and allowed investors to de-risk their positions in time. When they were finally issued, though, in September, 2008, they only accelerated the financial free-fall.

Finally, MBS and CDO were affected by a variety of political factors, some of which helped create, and others of which ultimately threatened the cash flow on which the securities depended. The primary factor that led to the creation of the securities was the easy credit maintained by the Fed after the dotcom bust (which by today's standards resulted in a relatively moderate and short-lived recession). Easy credit kept mortgage rates low, and combined with lax underwriting standards on the part of the mortgage industry, brought large numbers of first-time, often unqualified buyers into the housing market. There was little danger to the underwriters, however, because the resale of these questionable mortgages to the government-sponsored enterprises Fannie Mae and Freddie Mac—which in effect absolved the originators from the potential consequences of default—was all but guaranteed, *given political support for the expansion of home ownership.* Finally, many of the mortgages underwritten during the housing bubble required no documentation and no income verification, and by subsidizing such loans, some of which were guaranteed to fail over the long term, Fannie Mae and Freddie Mac helped set the stage for the inevitable cash-flow crunch that caused the value of mortgage-backed securities to collapse.

From a personal perspective, when my cleaning lady told me that she and her husband, who was a baggage handler at JFK, had just bought a $500,000 house in Nassau county, I knew something was about to go terribly wrong.

In retrospect, it now seems clear to all of us that the housing bubble was bound to burst, but as prices rose both buyers and sellers could still point to one irrefutable fact—with only a few, short-lived exceptions, housing prices in the United States had not fallen for more than 50 years. This unbroken trend, unfortunately, did not mean they never would. And when the inevitable reversal in valuation began, and then gathered speed in the spring of 2008, some MBS ratings changed from AAA to D in a single shot, an unprecedented event in the history of investment ratings. Months later, I asked the former managing director of one of the rating agencies how they managed to get it so wrong. His response: "We never thought that real estate values in the United States would drop so precipitously." De-risking your investments, then, requires a healthy skepticism of prevailing market psychology, and knowing that there is much that you don't know.

That managing director was not alone. And the unimaginable, sudden drop in housing prices—made all the more unsettling by investors' failure to consider the possibility—along with the subsequent disappearance of the market for mortgage-backed securities, made the value of the securities moot. All that mattered was the crisis in confidence, a crisis that essentially closed the credit markets to all participants. With confidence lost, and trust shattered, financial gridlock resulted.

And those who had not made plans, who had not carefully considered their present circumstances in light of their needs and wants, and who had not weighed the risks of their strategies accordingly—in other words, those who had not de-risked their positions— were lost.

Lessons for Individual Investors

At a recent conference, risk professionals took part in a poll on the causes and implications of the financial crisis. The results, not particularly surprising, but thought-provoking nonetheless, bear directly on individual risk management and decision making:

- Only three respondents believed that the primary cause of the financial crisis involved "global circumstances beyond anyone's control."
- More than half had major concerns about financial or market risks in advance of the crisis, but half of those felt unable to raise them with their colleagues or superiors.
- Most believed the greatest need for internal change is in organizational culture—not process. In other words, the crisis itself was avoidable; it was not an example of Greek tragedy, but of human error. And while many professionals had misgivings as the storm began to gather, few felt comfortable

discussing their concerns with colleagues or superiors.

• Finally, most risk management professionals believe that the procedures necessary to confront the next crisis are already in place; it's organizational culture—or risk management throughout the organization—that has to change.

It's also instructive to consider that the few financial institutions that survived the crisis more or less intact either realized their risk systems were not working properly, or were headed by individuals who did not underestimate the risks threatening their firms. John Thain, for example, the former COO of Merrill Lynch, could at one time have sold Merrill Lynch for $100 billion. Months later, during the worst days of the crisis, he was faced with a choice: Do I sell the company to the Bank of America for $50 billion and ensure that Merrill Lynch survives, or do I hold out, and if wrong, give my shareholders nothing? Thain, of course, decided to sell, but more than one CEO took the risk he wouldn't, and their shareholders paid the price. Again, to return to our earlier discussion of classical economics, this was an example of the ball not only being thrown off course by unprecedented shocks, but falling right off the table.

I wrote this book in order to prepare individual investors for the next crisis—because it's coming, sooner or later—and more specifically, to help them design specific procedures to protect their investments, their net worth, and most importantly, their lifestyles, when the next crisis arrives. Toward that end, based on my long career as an institutional risk manager, I will use these pages to present the fundamental principles of de-risking—principles that will provide a framework for decision making under four general headings: Assessment, the Rules of the Game, Decision Making, and Reevaluation.

Assessment

In general, human beings are more risk averse with their assets and more risk friendly with liabilities. This may be because we tend to significantly overvalue our assets, or because there is a natural, human emotional resistance to selling an asset for less than one has paid for it. Whatever the case may be, the first principle of decision making is to check your emotions at the door, and to be honest with yourself about what you do and don't know. Regarding the former, you do know what you want. As for the latter, make sure that you don't fool yourself into believing you know everything about how you decide to get it.

The Rules of the Game

You have to know the rules of the game, whether or not you intend to handle the day-to-day management of your investments. If you manage your own assets, a thorough understanding of the basic rules of the game is indispensable—but if you leave that management to others you will still need to understand the options your advisors propose, the risks those options entail, and to know enough about the process of investment to determine whether or not your requests have been faithfully executed. Furthermore, some decisions cannot be made for you. Only you, for instance, can determine your appetite for risk. Only you can clearly express your wishes, and ensure that those who handle your investments respect them. Only you, looking in from the outside, can determine whether the actions of those who handle your affairs are reasonably transparent, and only you, in the absence of such transparency, can demand it, or take your business elsewhere. And while you may not personally determine the distribution of your assets, you should be aware of the benefits of diversification—that is, a collection of counterbalanced risks—and the ability of such a strategy to reduce fluctuations in your portfolio. Internal checks and balances exist in all major financial institutions, but you too have a part to play. Finally, and perhaps most importantly, all of the rules of the game must be continually reviewed—not because they change, *but because conditions continually change around us.* When determining your risk appetite, for instance, you have not determined it for all time, but only for the present. And as circumstances change, so will that appetite.

Decision Making

Consider all alternatives before making decisions, but when you do decide, don't forget to consider exit strategies. Not all of your decisions will lead to favorable outcomes, but the *degree* to which things go wrong will depend on *how* you exit a given strategy. Attempt to include everyone you live and work with in the management of risk. Understand that it is your responsibility to investigate the reputations of those with whom you do business, whether they are active managers of your assets, or simply custodians. Frame your decision making in specific time frames, keeping in mind that your goals are certain to change. Finally, remember that it is always better to be approximately right than to be precisely wrong. Make decisions—don't sit and watch.

Reevaluation

Continually monitor the outcomes of your decisions, and of the decisions made on your behalf. Never stop asking questions. That said, understand your boundaries—which can also be defined as the limits of *your* responsibilities—and the boundaries of those who work for you. Finally, learn from your mistakes. Success frequently offers less information than failure. Learn to treat your mistakes, and the mistakes others make on your behalf, as charts you can use to successfully navigate the future.

Not long ago, walking along the beach, my wife and I ran into the owner of the local hardware store. The store had recently closed its doors, and we wanted to know why. He was more than willing to tell his story, and bent our ears for the better part of an hour as the three of us trudged along the shore.

The story was a simple one. His father had opened the store in 1930, built it up as a successful business, and had then turned it over to his son in 1980. Ten years later the son's mother died and his father remarried. When his father died, intestate, the store became the property of his second wife. The son, while disappointed, wasn't worried about losing his livelihood, because he knew his stepmother couldn't run the business without him. He never imagined, however, that his stepmother would simply sell the place, leaving him without a job. But that is exactly what she did. He considered himself a victim, but I couldn't believe he had allowed himself to be put in that position. He had made a series of poor decisions—not speaking to his father about the future of the business when he was an employee, not insisting on a share of the business once he began to run it, and finally, trusting his stepmother to continue the arrangement he had had with his father. The conclusion to the story wasn't by any means predictable, but when it happened, it happened quickly, and there was nothing he could do.

The following day, I happened to have lunch with a friend who has amassed a great fortune over the years, and as we ate I recounted a story of my own. I had donated a large sum of money to a certain charity with the understanding that the money would be used to start a specific program dear to my heart. A year or so later, I discovered that the charity had spent the bulk of the money according to their own lights, almost completely disregarding my instructions. My lunch partner was not sympathetic.

"This is all your fault," she said. "You didn't communicate your vision well, you didn't set up milestones, and you didn't monitor the charity's progress against them. And given your risk management expertise, you should have known better."

Only afterward did I realize that my story and the story of the hardware store owner had a lot in common. Both of us made a series of mistakes along the way, and when we found out what was happening, it was too late for either of us to do anything about it. He trusted that the business he and his father had built would continue indefinitely, and I failed to apply the principles of risk management I used at work to regulate my own charitable giving. In other words, we both failed at de-risking our plans.

So, while it's a little late for the man on the beach, and a little late for my most recent attempt at charitable giving, too, I'm hoping that this book, and through it a better understanding of the principles of risk management, will arrive in time for many of my readers to avoid similar mistakes. That, of course, will depend not only on this book's success in explaining these principles, but more importantly, on the willingness of readers to put them into action.

In short, those who believe in their ability to control certain well-defined outcomes will benefit from these pages, while those who are looking for someone to blame will not. For if the recent financial crisis can be considered a colossal, collective blunder—on the part of banks, investment management firms, government agencies, investment managers, ratings firms, *and* individual investors—rather than the result of uncontrollable economic forces, then there are lessons to be learned. And while those lessons will not forestall future economic crises, those who learn from them *can* improve their ability to weather the difficulties that lie between them and the realization of their plans.

A Story of Risk

On a fine spring day in the late 1970s which seemed to mirror their bright futures, Max and Rob put on their caps and gowns, marched into the auditorium with their classmates as "Pomp and Circumstance" blared from the tinny loudspeakers, nodded through two or three inspirational speeches, and graduated from college.

Their parents had as much, if not more, to celebrate than they did, but for different reasons. Rob's father and mother, watching breathlessly right up until the moment their son was handed a degree, sighed with relief. They had finally put the last of their four children through college, and that particular strain on their finances, at least, was over. Max's parents, who had had to contribute only the cost of books to their son's education, given the full academic scholarship the college had awarded him, watched with more pride than relief as Max crossed the stage. He was their middle child, sandwiched between two sisters, and was the first member of their family ever to graduate from college.

Max and Rob had been roommates since their sophomore year, when fate had thrown them together, and during the three years that followed they had become close friends, despite the striking differences in their backgrounds. Max had grown up in a public housing project in one of the outer boroughs of New York City, and had attended public schools. From the time he was a child he had excelled at math, and he was a capable chess player, too. His father, a decorated war hero, had returned from Europe in 1946 and found work as a truck driver, a job he kept for the rest of his working life. Max's mother stayed home to raise the family.

Rob had grown up in the suburbs north of the city, and had attended private schools. He had attended several of them, in fact. His academic achievements were—well, barely achieved. But he was a fine soccer player, and a popular boy. His father, a businessman, had changed businesses almost as often as his youngest son had changed prep schools, and for pretty much the same reasons. Rob's mother had never worked, although unlike Max's mother, she had left the housekeeping and the child rearing to the help.

Rob descended the stage clutching a degree in history, Max a degree in business. And at that precise moment, despite their years of friendship in college, they turned in completely different directions, directions that would remain remarkably consistent, despite the inevitable twists and turns of life, over the next 30 years. No one who knew them to that point would have been surprised. Rob was a handsome scoundrel, tall and blond-haired, while Max was shorter in stature, and wore glasses. But it wasn't their outward appearances that distinguished them, at least not so far as this story is concerned.

Max had seen his father work without pause his entire life. He was gone every morning long before his wife pried his children out of bed, and returned home just in time for dinner. He had provided for his family, and had never complained as he did it, but he never managed to put enough money away to take a real vacation, much less buy a house. When he died he left his family nothing—nothing, that is, but cherished memories, and a model of manhood that Max would attempt to emulate for the rest of his life.

Rob had watched his father work, too. In particular, he had watched him work his way through the money Rob's grandfather had left the family. His grandfather had been born into the middle class, but by virtue of hard work, and a little luck in the form of the Second World War, had made his fortune supplying uniforms to the army. After the war, when uniforms began to last a little longer than they had in the 1940s, he branched out into textile machinery. The success of that business, however, declined as European manufacturers recovered and once again began to dominate the market. Just the same, Max's grandfather, in large part due to his wartime connections, kept that business barely profitable until the early 1960s, when he retired and put his eldest son, Rob's father, in charge. Within a year the company filed for bankruptcy protection.

Who can say why some save and others spend, but Rob's father was clearly a member of the latter group. And even if he hadn't been, his wife was an accomplished spender herself, and grew better with practice. (For the purposes of accuracy I suppose I should say his *second* wife, since his first marriage lasted only a few months, which was just long enough for his first wife to empty out a few safety deposit boxes and then hail a cab to her lawyer's office.)

But Rob and Max's parents aren't the protagonists of this story— their sons are. And as I wrote above, this story concerns their approach to risk, and that is what drives this narrative. Our two young friends had, in fact, developed their risk appetites long before they crossed the stage to receive their degrees, and those appetites were as different and enduring as day is from night. Rob had only one thing on his mind—how he could manage to maintain the $250,000 trust fund his grandfather had left him, because if he failed at that task, he would have to do the unthinkable—make a living. Max, on the other hand, had waited four years to get to work, and he had his first paycheck spent well before he'd earned it. He'd been looking at a little company trading on the NASDAQ, and thought it had room to move.

PART | 1

ASSESSMENT

Risk Principle | 1

KNOW WHERE YOU ARE

"You've got to be very careful if you don't know where you're going,
because you might not get there."
—Yogi Berra

M ost of us move through our lives oblivious to what is happening around us. We focus on the events of the day, or sometimes, only on the events of the moment. This tendency is not all bad; it allows us to focus, and for many of us it's the only way we are able to get anything done at all. It is also a form of myopia, however, one that prevents us from seeing past the walls of the present and getting a glimpse of the future.

This is not only an intellectual or a psychological tendency—the limits of our senses themselves keep us from being aware of much that goes on around us, and this too, more often than not, is a good thing. Imagine, for example, if we were able to hear the sounds of the cells in our bodies endlessly dividing themselves—the roar would deafen us. In fact, it seems as if the ability to think clearly is dependent on a certain level of sensory deprivation—on a tunnel vision, on the construction of a sensory cocoon of sorts. For this reason most of us avoid noise as we work, and going home at night are aware only of those things that have an immediate effect on our senses, like the weather, or the presence or absence of sunlight. Again, there are advantages to such an approach—after all, to look too far ahead is to look past those things that are right in front of you—but it is equally true that to remain stubbornly shortsighted robs us of whatever chance we have to visualize what lies ahead.

Our first sensations, in fact, at the beginning of every day, are of our immediate surroundings. Though the process may occur subconsciously our eyes first take in the familiar sights of our bedrooms, or of the hotel room we entered the evening before, establishing our location. This, it seems, is our mind's way of telling us that in order to know what we're doing, and where we might go, we first have to know *where* we are.

At first, this may appear to be a contradiction—that is, the notion that one can focus both on short-term events *and* long-term plans—but our lives are full of such inconsistencies. The trick lies in knowing how to change your field of vision when the time is right, first studying the details, and then stepping back to look at the big picture. Without the details, after all, the big picture doesn't exist at all.

During the fall of 2008, as our nation's financial system staggered and nearly collapsed, my staff and I worked from early in the morning until late at night evaluating counterparty risk. The volume of data was unprecedented, volatility was off the charts, and the pressure to keep up with rapidly unfolding events was relentless. Each day brought some fresh disaster, and with it the need to make yet another round of important decisions. Even during the worst of times, though, my staff and I were never truly overwhelmed, because we never failed to keep up with the torrent of data flowing across our computer monitors, no matter how long it took. Thus, no matter how many twists and turns the markets had taken, we always knew where we stood.

Compare this approach to your own. You know what you earn, but do you know what you spend? You know what you have, but do you know what you owe? Do you know what your portfolio is worth today? Do you know whether or not it's leveraged, and most importantly, what risks are involved in your positions?

Nothing is more unsettling—at least in the world of finance—than being unable to determine the value of a position at any given moment. Without knowing the value of your holdings you can't manage your present, or plan for your future. For that reason, even during the toughest market days, experienced investment advisors continue to watch their screens, but vow to do nothing—nothing emotional, that is. They are able to stand at ease, while the events of the day knock others off their feet, because they believe in the essential soundness of their positions. They believe in their game plans. And as a result, they can check their emotions at the door every morning, settle in behind their desks, and calmly continue the research on which their long-term decisions are based. The day's events may move the markets, but those events don't move them. And they are able to remain detached because to the extent possible they have *already* de-risked their portfolios.

The economic events of 2008, however, tested even the most battle-hardened veterans in the financial world, and so during the six months between the fire sale of Bear Stearns and the collapse of Lehman Brothers my colleagues and I used a number of techniques to ground ourselves, and to help us check our emotions. One of my favorites was the following: "Okay, everyone, imagine we're all watching as a hydrogen bomb is dropped. We're not at ground zero, we're 20 miles away, and while we're going to survive the initial explosion, we're still not safe from the after effects. So, let's keep calm, get to work, and distance ourselves from the problem."

Maintain some perspective, in other words, but be sure you're still able to see what's going on day to day. That will allow you to stay out in front of events, instead of following them.

Stay Out in Front of Events

John Opel, CEO of IBM from 1981 to 1985, was once asked about the circumstances that led to his resignation. As President, CEO, and finally as Chairman of the Board, Opel had overseen the mainframe giant's unsuccessful foray into personal computers, while vigorously defending the company against anti-trust charges. During that period Opel himself had asked Bill Gates to develop the IBM-PC's first operating system, but he inexplicably allowed Microsoft to license that software for sales to other companies—in other words, IBM underwrote the development of the software that would one day be used by its competitors. In fact, on Opel's watch, IBM not only didn't monitor the strategies of its competitors in the fledgling market for personal computers, it flatly refused the requests of its own scientists to monitor its competitors' progress. As a result, the company was unable to keep pace with the rapid-fire innovations of Microsoft, Apple, and the other manufacturers of PCs. Describing his own downfall, Opel said that he could "never get out in front of events."

When a crisis occurs—whether it involves your business or your personal life—you need to think ten steps ahead, the way a chess player does. You need to be as far out in front of events as you possibly can. That way, you'll have time to get in position before adverse events occur—and perhaps even more importantly, while opportunities still exist.

Look Around

Knowing where you are also involves knowing what's going on around you. If you're on a sailboat, it's not enough to know that your sails are in good condition, your rigging is taut, and your hull is freshly painted—not if a storm is gathering on the horizon. A structurally sound house is another example of an assessment that becomes meaningless when taken out of context. What does it matter that your house is solidly built, and rests on a sound foundation, if the ground beneath it begins to shake?

In both cases decisions made long before the storm strikes, or the earthquake hits, will greatly affect the degree to which changing circumstances will either leave you in control—or overwhelm you. The sailor can, for instance, pay greater attention to the weather report before casting off his lines, or before plotting his course. And depending on the results of his research, he may choose the wisest course, and leave his boat tied to its mooring. The house builder can pay more attention to underlying geological conditions before choosing his site, or to the stability of the soil, or the frequencies of brush fires in the area. We will turn to these sorts of decisions in our discussion of Risk Principle 3, but for now it's enough to say that being able to determine your position is only half the job—the other half of the job involves monitoring and forecasting the conditions around you. Here too, one's appetite for risk comes into play, another topic I'll discuss at greater length later in this book.

During the fall of 2008 this sort of forethought became especially important. In addition to our positions themselves, my staff and I also paid careful attention to how closely certain counterparties— that is, firms with whom we did business—monitored their collateral, and how aggressively they made margin calls (i.e., requests for additional funds to back up our positions, due to fluctuations in their market value).

Margin calls are usually a source of concern to those receiving them, but we used the calls, which we had no trouble meeting, to gauge the level of the *caller's* liquidity. In fact, as the crisis worsened we found we could measure the weakness of our counterparties by the speed with which they made these calls. And acting on this insight, we reduced our exposure to those firms, in case the crisis worsened, and they were unable to satisfy *their* capital requirements.

This was but one insight, and only part of our overall approach to maintaining a sense of where we were. It's as if we were playing poker, and were sitting across the table from someone who had a pair of aces showing, and yet was sweating profusely. Clearly something was bothering him about his down cards. Again, the important thing is to continually gather information, sometimes from unconventional sources, so that you can stay ahead of events.

One of the best pre-crisis examples of this approach, at least on the managerial level, involved Alan Mulally and the Ford Motor Company. For lack of a better term, it might be called "defensive financing." Anticipating tighter credit, Mulally directed Ford to borrow approximately $23 billion *before* the financial crisis began, in essence mortgaging the company's future *to ensure it would have one.* Investors and analysts were not impressed, and neither General Motors nor Chrysler followed suit. A year later, however, Mulally was proven right.

The collapse of housing prices caused credit markets to seize up, and caused homeowners to stop spending—and that, in turn, hurt car sales. And plummeting sales made it difficult for auto manufacturers to pay their suppliers, to loan money to their dealers, *and* extend credit to the few willing buyers left in the market for a car. Higher gasoline prices and rising unemployment further curtailed sales. But by thinking proactively—that is, by getting out in front of events—Mulally was able to spare his company the restrictions of government aid, to say nothing of a Chapter 11 filing, something neither GM nor Chrysler were able to do. The results speak for themselves. In 2009, three years after Ford's round of defensive borrowing, and despite its triple-C credit rating, the company was still able to find willing buyers for three separate bond offerings—each at a successively lower yield. The market's take on Ford in 2009? The stock price tripled.

To put it a different way, GM and Chrysler thought they knew where they stood, but events proved them wrong. Only Ford— thanks to Mulally's decision to scrutinize not only the needs of the company, but also the state of the economy, and then to stay out in front of events—succeeded in defending itself.

Liquidity

Assessing your present position also involves judging your ability to *access* your holdings—or in other words, determining the liquidity of your holdings. This isn't as significant a factor if you have staying power in the form of cash on hand, but even that sort of protection came under fire shortly after Lehman Brothers failed, and money market funds with significant holdings in Lehman were forced to "break the buck."*

Even in good times liquidity can be hard to measure, primarily because it is usually based on historical transaction volumes. If, for example, you wanted to unload a large block of stock, selling it all on the same day might cause the price to fall. As a result complex models have been developed that factor in the average number of shares traded, estimates of supply, and potential demand. Taken together, these numbers are used to determine the potential drop in price based on the size of the transaction.

But not even these models are set in stone. Some studies have shown that as equity shares drop precipitously there is a rise in liquidity. Why? Because different buyers enter the market at different price points. At $20 per share you may have demand from institutional investors, while at $5 per share the stock will be bought by "vultures," or investors who buy when prices drop significantly below book value.

When volatility is dramatic, however, nearly all investors move to the sidelines, awaiting signs of stability. This makes determining liquidity especially difficult. Think of it this way: Say you own your home outright, and decide to sell it. If you put a For Sale sign on your lawn at 3:00 in the morning, how many buyers will appear? So, liquidity has an added dimension beyond historical transaction volumes—it has a time frame, one that may limit your ability to

---

* Money market funds, regulated by the Securities and Exchange Commission (SEC), are required to hold highly rated, short-term debt in order to maintain a fixed net asset value (NAV) of $1 per share.

convert your assets into cash *when* you want to convert them. For that reason institutional traders who want to liquidate large positions often trade out of them over the course of a few days to keep from dramatically affecting the price in a single session.

During liquidity crunches it is extremely important for large institutions—like those who manage your assets—to maintain dedicated lines of credit. For example, if a hedge fund receives numerous requests for redemptions, managers will usually sell their most liquid positions to raise cash. As a result the remaining investors are left holding more concentrated, illiquid positions. If, however, a fund has dedicated bank credit lines—lines that a bank cannot close in a crisis—it may be able to handle redemptions without being forced to sell not only its most liquid positions, but its illiquid positions as well—which almost always sell well below their value.

This issue also bears on investment strategy compliance—that is, the degree to which your advisor adheres both to your general desires and your specific game plan—about which I'll have more to say in Risk Principle 2. My discussion in the Introduction of this book regarding "dealers" markets and valuations for MBS and CDO is a good example. These instruments had an observable value before the credit markets seized up, but once the markets for those instruments froze it was almost impossible to know what they were worth. Auction rate securities (ARS) are a perfect example. In short, ARS were debt instruments composed of corporate or municipal bonds with variable interest rates that were frequently recalculated at regularly scheduled "Dutch auctions." Presented as highly liquid alternatives to cash holdings, and paying higher returns than money market funds, they too became illiquid when the usual bidders vanished during the credit crisis.

The value of your assets can also fluctuate wildly during a crisis, even if the underlying value—say the value of the cash flow underlying MBS—remains the same. To some extent, given the continuing instability of housing prices, that confusion still exists today. But on the 25th of every month the firms that service MBS and CDO publish their cash flows. And then the analysts take a few days to pour over the numbers. And then the prices change. And if either you, or the firm that manages your money, has holdings of this kind, you'd do well to watch those numbers too.

Actively Seek the Opinions of Others

In addition to staying out in front of events, seeking the opinions of others is a critical part of the process of finding out where you are. Throughout my career, I have always maintained my own personal Board of Directors. That group is composed of the men and women I've met throughout my career who have been able to look past what I was saying and tell me what I was really thinking—sometimes before I knew it myself. All brilliant in their own right, and each of them successful in their own spheres, I make a point of bouncing my thoughts off each one of them whenever I have an important personal business decision to make. The process, in fact, is similar to that which every effective CEO follows with his own Board. Seeking objective opinions from people you know and trust can help separate emotion from a rational consideration of the facts, and either confirm your thinking or provide constructive criticism.

I seek alternative views just as vigorously, especially of those of so-called dissidents. Oftentimes those who are sharply opposed to the conventional wisdom—be it yours, or that held by others—are able to provide information we either haven't considered, or that we tended to discount. Sometimes their thinking is not truly contrarian, but simply ahead of its time. In the early 1990s, when I was responsible for enterprise risk at Citicorp, I called in Paul Krugman to speak at our quarterly risk meeting. At the time the future Nobel Prize winner questioned the novelty of the so-called East Asian economic "Tigers," arguing that the growth of Asian economies was due *not* to a particularly Asian "miracle," but the more traditional and often transitory factors of increased capital investment and rising labor force participation. After a great deal of discussion we at Citibank decided he was right—at least in the short term—and took extraordinary measures to reduce our exposure in Thailand, Indonesia, and Korea, some of the countries hit hardest by the Asian financial crisis of 1997. Today everyone listens to what Krugman has to say—whether or not they agree with him—but 15 years ago, as hard as it is to believe today, he was a dissident.

We were also willing to listen to Krugman because we accepted the inevitability of change—that is, despite conventional wisdom to the contrary, Eastern economies would experience business cycles similar to those in Western economies—and that in order to stay ahead of events we had to be willing to close the door on the past.

Move Forward

During my years at Citibank I also often took part in Creditors Committees (formed when companies with whom we did business went broke). The process usually began in a large conference room, and included representatives from other banks that had lent the bankrupt company money. No matter the circumstances—that is, whether the bankruptcy was the result of market forces, changes in consumer sentiment, or outright fraud—the meetings usually began with everyone screaming about the dishonesty or incompetence of the bankrupt company's management. After allowing everyone to vent, I would call for order and then begin the meeting by saying: "Ladies and gentlemen, we are where we are, and the only relevant issue is where we can go from here."

In other words, the past is often an obstacle to those who wish to move forward. Think, for a moment, of the Old Testament, the first line of which reads: "In the beginning . . . ." In some versions of the Bible the first letter of the word "beginning" is capitalized and illuminated—that is, ornately decorated—and the "B" has a diagonal line through it, almost as if the artist meant to remind us that the creation itself was a break from the past—that is, from the formless void that preceded it.

Data and Direction

Years before I went to work for Citibank, I began my career in the audit division at Price Waterhouse & Co.—now PricewaterhouseCoopers—eventually moving over to the consulting division. One of the lasting memories I have of those long ago days involves a job I oversold—in fact, a job I oversold so badly that I had to work all night to deliver what I had promised. At the time I shared a small, windowless office with another consultant, and I stayed there at my desk until the following morning. When my boss arrived, around 8:00 a.m., he found me still hard at work. There wasn't a square inch of free space on my desk, the papers were piled about two feet high, and a layer of cigarette smoke hung below the ceiling. Far from congratulating me on my work ethic, my boss started to ask me questions, each one more detailed than the one that preceded it. I felt like he was taking me apart bone by bone, but he was just doing what he had to in order to understand what I had been doing—he was just reviewing the facts I had gathered.

Once he had the information he needed, he stopped interrogating me and began to discuss the project. But once he had finished he didn't leave. Instead, he sat down in my absent colleague's chair, put his feet on top of a stack of papers on my desk, took a sip of coffee and then said: "Damn it, Martin! When I walk past your office in the morning I don't want to see you working like a miner in a tunnel, I want to see you staring out the window. I want to see you *thinking* your way out of a problem instead of trying to *dig* your way out."

I knew better than to point out that my office had no window, but I knew what he meant. Yes, you have to know the facts first, but they are only building blocks used to design a plan of action. Put another way, you have to know where you are before you can figure out how to go anywhere else.

A Story of Risk: Part 1

We pick up with Max and Rob not where we left off in the Introduction to this book, when the two of them had finally escaped the tender cruelties of higher education, but five years later, as their futures began to unfold. Those five years, I'm sorry to say, had not been particularly kind to either of them—at least in financial terms.

A large part of their bad luck stemmed from factors far outside their control. To begin with, they had had the misfortune to enter the working world in the late 1970s while the U.S. economy suffered from the twin evils of stagnant growth and high inflation—or stagflation. Remedial action on the part of the government—in particular the decision to raise interest rates in order to stifle inflation—made the economic situation even worse. They weren't the only ones in trouble; the national unemployment rate, not much higher than 6 percent on the day they graduated, had climbed to over 10 percent. The economic malaise, however, while good for neither of them, affected Max and Rob in entirely different ways—and that difference was the result of their differing appetites for risk.

Rob, as I pointed out in the Introduction, had a very small appetite for risk. As a boy he had watched his father fail to add to the family fortune, and succeed at squandering much of what his grandfather had left him, not least of which was a thriving business. Rob was determined not to make the same mistake. Therefore, as soon as he turned 25, and took control of his trust fund, he made certain that it was safely invested in a mix of corporate bonds and Treasury bills, which weren't subject to the wild fluctuations of the stock market, and paid dividends besides. He went to work for his father's stock broker, rented an apartment with a doorman in a new high-rise on the Upper East Side of Manhattan, and made friends quickly, many of them bartenders.

In different times, say 30 years earlier, his plan, just like his bonds, would have paid generous dividends. But he had failed to consider one critical element—inflation. The year he took control of his trust fund inflation was running about 6 percent. Two years later it had climbed northward of 13 percent, and while the combination of his earnings as a stock broker and the interest income from his investments paid his expenses, the relative value of his trust fund declined.

He paid little attention to it, though, as long as it looked more or less like it did the last time he checked his statement. It was true, the co-op he had considered buying only two years earlier was now out of his reach, but he slept easily at night, knowing that he still had six figures to his name, an American Express Gold card in his wallet, and owed nothing. In short, after assessing his situation, and his prospects, he liked what he saw, and wanted to keep seeing it.

Max had settled in New York too, but lived a world away and a long train ride from the Upper East Side. He had moved back in with his parents and sisters right after he graduated from college and had immediately begun to study for his CPA. He drove a cab at night to pay his share of the bills at home, and to cover the cost of his studies. Two years later, shortly after he passed his exam, he rented a fourth-floor walk-up in lower Manhattan, against his mother's wishes. Why pay for an apartment, she asked him, when he had a perfectly good room to sleep in as it was? His sisters, at least whenever they were out of earshot of his mother, encouraged him to live his own life, perhaps because they knew that if he moved out they'd each have a room of their own for the first time in their lives.

Max figured the time had come to make his own way in the world. He had his college degree, his CPA, and boundless ambition, fueled by the inescapable fear that if he didn't work as hard as he could he'd never escape the life his parents had lived. He had virtually nothing in the way of assets, but he'd already made—and lost—a few thousand dollars in the stock market. A couple months after he started driving the cab he'd managed to put aside $500, and he promptly invested all of it in the penny stock that had caught his eye in college. Within weeks the stock took off like a rocket to the moon, and he began to wonder if he weren't wasting his time studying to become an accountant. The stock never made it past the Earth's gravity, however, much less to the moon. In fact, it crashed back to Earth far more quickly than it had climbed. The experience didn't bother him—at least not for more than a week or two—but he never again considered interrupting his studies. He studied even harder, in fact, but kept his eye on the NASDAQ the whole time. He wasn't interested in the staid New York Stock Exchange. The blue chips were for singles hitters, and he was looking for a home run, so it was strictly over-the-counter stocks for him. By the time he passed his CPA exam, and was offered a job at a large accounting firm, he was ready to try again.

Risk Principle | 2

KNOW WHAT YOU
DON'T KNOW

"Real knowledge is to know the extent of one's ignorance."
—Confucius

An expert diver takes a beginner on his first dive. The beginner takes deep breaths, and then, as his heart beats faster and faster, jumps in feet first. The expert, who understands the principles of buoyancy, knows that full lungs have the same effect as a life preserver—that is, they will stop your descent. Therefore, the expert breathes normally and follows his student into the water.

As the beginner struggles to descend the expert grabs one of his shoulders and guides him down. As they continue lower the beginner, who has forgotten that his ears need to be equalized by squeezing his nostrils and blowing through his nose—to expel the air in his eustachian tube—feels as if his ears are about to explode. The expert, seeing what's happening, mimes the appropriate motion, and the beginner follows his lead.

As they near the bottom the expert squirts some air into his buoying compensator to become *buoyancy neutral*. Having done so, the expert begins to float near the bottom, almost as if he were suspended in air. The beginner, who once again has forgotten the instructions he was given, cannot stop his descent and crashes into the sandy bottom.

The expert works to settle the beginner, showing him how to take long, slow, deep breaths to preserve his oxygen. As the expert, completely at home far beneath the surface of the water, checks the beginner's oxygen gauge, the beginner is startled by the strange world around him. Shimmering schools of fish flash past him, and giant corals of varying colors glow in the filtered sunlight. Spellbound, the beginner has no idea that as they swim the expert is also checking his dive computer to calculate the amount of time they can stay on the bottom without taking too much nitrogen into their bodies.

And so it goes throughout the beginner's first dive, an experience for which his imagination could not possibly have prepared him. The sound of his own breathing, and the sight of the bubbles rising to the surface, is exhilarating. His buoyancy, and the ease with which his flippers move him through the water, is otherworldly. The expert, of course, has been there before. He knows all about underwater breathing equipment, gas mixes, support systems, compression chambers, and is able to diagnose and treat all common diving injuries and illnesses. He knows everything the beginner does not know, but the beginner knew one thing, at least—he had no business being down there on his own.

In order to figure out where we are going, then, we have to continually ask ourselves where we are. Where are we in our personal relationships, where are we in the span of our careers, where do we stand financially? To do this with any accuracy requires research, but it is equally important to acknowledge the *limits* of our knowledge. Learn what you can, but keep in mind that there is a great deal you don't know, and you ignore that hidden knowledge at your own peril. In this sense, you de-risk your plans by leaving room for the unknown. And then you keep your eyes and ears open, and ask everyone you know for their input.

Or let's look at in another way, by asking the following question: When does a problem become a problem? The answer? Long before it is recognized as such—or put another way, while it is still an unknown. For that reason, basing your decisions solely on what you know, on what you can see, or put your hands on, is inherently dangerous. You'll never be far wrong if you presume that something you don't know about, or more likely many things you don't know about, are going on out there.

A serious illness—say any one of a number of cancers—is an excellent example. It's not truly a problem at its outset, because you don't know it exists. You go about your business, you live your life, and you make your plans. You presume that each day will be followed by another, just as it always has. And all the while the cancer cells multiply. The problem begins once the first symptoms appear, or when you begin to feel the effects of the tumor. Then, within a few days, although the cancer may have been growing inside you for months, you find yourself sitting on an examination table in a sterile room, listening to a man wearing a white coat with a stethoscope around his neck. He's holding a thin manila folder in one hand, and he does not have good news.

Risk, as I pointed out earlier, is most accurately measured and managed by people, not mathematical models, *because the latter never know what they do not know.* This is as true of health risks as it is of financial risk. Advances in mathematics and computer technology, however, have given many of us a false sense of security. They have given rise to a high-tech vision of risk management, with a corporate risk manager sitting in front of a series of flat-panel monitors across which the risk data for the entire company streams. This fictional version of a risk manager keeps his hands on his computer keyboard, watching as market conditions change, and alerts the company's portfolio managers as certain risk thresholds are reached, whether high or low. A computer program then automatically directs the trading desk to adjust the level of the company's risk accordingly.

As technologically satisfying as such a vision of risk management may be, we must keep in mind that most mathematical risk models do not *adapt* to data; instead, they are limited by the nature of their inputs, necessarily excluding more data than they include, and are then directed to perform predetermined mathematical tasks. Such models may take historic trends and project them forward, or they may consider changes in outcomes caused by single variables. When such risk models were used to examine the condition of Lehman Brothers, for instance, they most likely projected the status quo—that is, the relative stability the investment bank had enjoyed since it first began to underwrite public offerings at the turn of the twentieth century.

What those models were unable to do, it is easy enough to see in hindsight, was to project the consequences of events outside their range of possibilities. Think about it this way. People file into a movie theater through wide, easily navigated corridors, but if a fire breaks out they all run for the fire exits, which are just wide enough for a couple people to squeeze through at a time. The models, in other words, didn't take into account the possibility that everyone would try to get out at the same time, and that not all of them would make it.

That belief in the status quo of Lehman Brothers was solidly supported by the firm's history. By 2008, more than 160 years after the company was founded, Lehman Brothers had weathered the Civil War, two World Wars, the Great Depression, and a bitter succession battle (after the retirement of the last member of the Lehman family). Even after being sold, in the mid-1980s, to Shearson American Express—at about the same time John Opel completed his stewardship of IBM—Lehman Brothers managed to stay on its feet. And ten years later, after the leadership of American Express decided to divest itself of noncore businesses, the company was spun off again as Lehman Brothers Holding Company, Inc.

Despite its storied past—the company underwrote the initial offerings of F.W. Woolworth, Studebaker, and B.F. Goodrich, to name but a few—its twenty-first-century risk models were not designed for a catastrophic event like the collapse of the real estate market. As early as August of 2007 it had closed the doors of its subprime-mortgage unit—BNC Mortgage—and had written down losses in excess of $50 million (including goodwill), but it was too little too late.

In 2008, Lehman Brothers still held large positions in subprime tranches of the MBS it had underwritten, and as the real estate market and then the financial markets crashed it was forced to sell assets—the value of which had plummeted—in order to cover its losses. In normal times the misfortunes of an industry titan like Lehman might have led to its acquisition by a healthier competitor, but in 2008 no company was safe from the downward spiral in values. Such a change in the environment, at least up to that point, had been unimaginable—that is, unknowable.

One cannot blame the maker of the model. There is very little historical data for systemic economic problems, to say nothing of the liquidity issues that arise afterward, and therefore Lehman Brothers' models were only as good as the data on which they were based. This brings us back to our risk manager of the future, who banks on the reliability of his company's data and the ability of his computer programs to measure risk and correct positions automatically. In hindsight there is little doubt that Lehman Brothers would have been well served by a risk manager from the past too—a gray-haired, caffeine addict with a paunch, who, if line managers had walked into his office saying they wanted to invest in more real estate would have said, without so much as looking at a spreadsheet, "No thanks, I've already got my fill."

Most of the financial institutions that survived the subprime meltdown, for instance, had leadership with experience in Latin America in the 1980s, or with Asia in the 1990s—experiences that couldn't be programmed into more modern risk models fed by streams of purely economic data. The lesson is clear now, of course—seek as broad a variety of information as possible, tap the experiences of those with whom you work, look backward as well as forward, and be wary of overdependence on any one analytical tool—especially mathematical models. Again, my point is not that such models should be abandoned, but that they are only one tool of the many available, and in times of trouble a wise man will turn the toolbox upside down to make sure he uses everything in it. I'll return to this topic in greater detail in Risk Principle 8 when I turn to the mechanics of decision making.

A crystal ball, unfortunately, is not one of the tools in the box. But that doesn't mean abandoning a reasonable doubt about someone else's assessment—an assessment that will almost certainly *not* include all available, or pertinent, information. Sometimes this is the result of simple laziness, and sometimes it is the result of historical bias—but it is almost always the result of failing to acknowledge what you don't know.

IBM's decision to ignore the growth of personal computers in the 1980s—or perhaps better yet, their decision to downplay the potential for such growth—is an especially apt example, and particularly ironic given the company's global dominance in computing. At the time the technology of personal computers was in its infancy, as was the market for such devices. And lest you suspect this to be yet another example of one company's over-reliance on computer modeling, that is not the case. IBM didn't rely on mathematical models, they held strategy meetings to determine what the likely future of this segment of the market would be. The problem arose because they considered the fledgling industry in light of their own company's history—that is, by IBM's attempts to manufacture ever larger and faster mainframe computers. As a result, they concluded that within the next decade or so only about 60,000 PCs would be sold worldwide. That's right. IBM's strategists predicted that the *global* market for PCs would amount to approximately 60,000 units, and the company made both its manufacturing decisions, and its strategic decisions, on the basis of that projection.

Of course as everyone now knows—or at least anyone with an Internet connection—tens of millions of PCs were sold in that decade, and not only the world of computing, but the entire developed world was forever transformed. In 1980, however, nearly everyone at IBM trusted an utterly inappropriate decision model, because the company couldn't figure out how people would *use* their PCs. And no one stopped for a moment to consider that perhaps they didn't understand the potential of the PC—that perhaps they didn't know.

I said earlier that *nearly* everyone at IBM trusted an utterly inappropriate decision model, and I made that statement because I don't know for sure that everyone did. Why don't I know? Because IBM's upper-level management never even sought the advice of its *own* scientists. What's more, they explicitly forbade their research scientists from monitoring the advances of their competitors—and by that I mean both their competitors' software and their hardware. In those days, you couldn't find a PC clone in any IBM lab.

Nor did their strategists consider the effects of pricing—most likely because the company's goal at the time was to *increase* price, along with the performance of their flagship product, the mainframe, and so they never considered the possibility that if PCs were to become reasonably priced, people would *figure out* uses for them. And that, of course, is exactly what happened.

This discussion reminds me of a PRIMIA C-Suite meeting I attended in the summer of 2007. During that meeting, the Chief Risk Officers of the major financial firms spent their time discussing the issues of the day, and asking each other for advice. Senior executives of Fannie Mae and Freddie Mac happened to be there, and they asked us, as a group, how much capital we thought they should maintain on their balance sheets. By this they meant capital as a percentage of the total debt they held.

In framing the question they stipulated that it did not make sense—at least to them—to consider extreme events, because the amount of capital required would be impossible to maintain. I argued that capital requirements shouldn't be determined on the basis of *known* risks, but for *unknown* risks—that is, for risks that were by their nature unseen—and by that measure both Fannie and Freddie were dangerously undercapitalized. In short, Fannie and Freddie's management had decided they wouldn't even *consider* the risks associated with an extreme economic downturn, because *they were so dangerously undercapitalized.* I lost the argument that day, but as sorry as I am to say it, history proved me right.

A large part of the problem with Fannie Mae and Freddie Mac's decision making, at least from my point of view, stemmed from their inability, or their outright refusal, to take a more holistic view of their businesses. Had they looked at their entire operation—that is, studied the *nature* of their business—they would have had a better sense of how they needed to manage the risks they had assumed, the capital they had deployed, and the strategies they had pursued. In other words, they could have de-risked their business model.

Any given strategy, for example, consumes a certain amount of capital. A commercial bank focused on the transactions business requires far less capital than an investment firm concentrating on principal trading. Why? Because each strategy has *different risks*. Clearly, there is significantly less risk involved in performing delivery versus payment transactions than in taking investment positions for your own account. But only by taking a more holistic view, thinking simultaneously of risk, capital, and strategy, can you reach the best decision. For Fannie and Freddie that would have meant taking into account just how thin their margins were, and how few additional foreclosures it would take—that is, above the long-term, historic average—to upend their business model.

Put yet another way, businesses have strategies, those strategies create risks, and managing those risks requires a certain amount of capital. Therefore, if you don't understand the business strategy, you can't understand the risks, and won't be able to calculate the appropriate level of capital. Consider the following simplistic example.

One summer in New York two unemployed construction workers decide to go into the watermelon business. It's hot out, and wherever they go they see people eating watermelon. So they decide to drive a truck down to Florida, buy watermelons for 50 cents each, and then drive back to New York and sell them for the same price. After they'd made a few trips they realized that things weren't working out, but they couldn't figure out why. Finally, after thinking it over, one of them said to the other: What we need is a *bigger* truck.

What they needed, of course, was a different business model, one that took into account the spread between cost and sale price. Given their model, the bigger their truck, and the more trips they took, the more money they would *lose*. Again, the point is that no one can manage risk without first understanding the underlying business model. Experts as well as amateurs often fail to consider this fundamental concept, as the following story demonstrates.

Early in my career, as part of my work for PWC's consulting division, I often provided litigation support. This involved everything from expert testimony on financial matters to helping lawyers assemble the complicated financial information for specific cases. As part of one particular assignment, I was asked to review the claims of a shipyard against the U.S. Military Sealift Command (MSC), a component of the U.S. Navy. Manned by civilians, the MSC provides maritime transportation and support for the Department of Defense (DOD), using both naval vessels and chartered merchant marine ships.

The case in question involved a Continuing Overhead Claim brought on the part of a private shipyard, asking for additional charges for the time, or "overtime," during which U.S. Navy ships occupied space in the yard. The shipyard contended that the Navy should bear a portion of the cost of their continuing overhead, or their fair share of the cost of maintaining the shipyard's infrastructure. For more than four years the government's lawyer had argued the claim on the basis of the hourly overtime *cost*, claiming that it was so outrageously high that the Navy should not pay it. When I reviewed the pertinent financial information, I quickly realized that the Navy's attorney, who worked for a prestigious law firm, was arguing the wrong point. The objection should have been based on the following question: Would the shipyard have incurred these costs *whether or not* the Navy's ships were in the yard? If the answer was yes, then the Navy should be liable only for those costs not allocated against other ships in the yard at that time.

My point is that this approach, while obvious to a trained accountant, had not occurred to the highly paid, experienced lawyer contesting the claim. The lawyer was well-educated and hardworking but simply did not understand the salient point of this particular dispute. Nor, apparently, had it occurred to him that there might be something he didn't know about general accounting practices for these sorts of costs. Again, successful risk management should not depend *solely* on either computer models or human judgment. Instead, the research phase should include as many sources of information as possible, given the time you have to make the decision, and should always include a healthy skepticism as to whether all the relevant information has been found—since no one can, and no one does, know everything.

Keep in mind, however, that to acknowledge that you "know you don't know" does not mean that you will one day understand all things. That day will never come, but your willingness to consider the possibility that there are facts, forces, and potentialities of which you are unaware is a valuable perspective in and of itself.

I'll end this section with one more example, which involves gathering information from both "black box" and "white box" accounting systems. Black box accounting is concerned with generally accepted standards and regulatory requirements. These include the specific methodologies that result in the numbers published in financial statements (or the GAAP required by the FASB). White box accounting instead includes factors critical to the successful *management* of the business. Most managers, for instance, don't understand the intricacies of GAAP. But any good line manager is able to tell you what he's monitoring—that is, the supply chain, orders, or changing workforce needs. The point is this: When you study the business model, don't forget to track the numbers that represent the vital signs of the business.

For example, after reviewing the financial statements of a public company in which you want to invest, you might try to find out which numbers the CEO tracks from day to day—or in other words, the numbers he or she considers the most vital signs of the business. As important as the black box numbers are, white box accounting is often more predictive of the health of a business, and more importantly, the potential for problems.

A Good Example

Demographics are as good an example of this principle—that is, of knowing what you don't know—as anyone is ever likely to find. In short, while we don't know precisely what the future is going to be like, certain demographic trends can help us fill in many of the blanks. Global population trends, in fact, are an excellent example of a widely studied, frequently discussed body of knowledge that still fails to show up on most people's radar. We pay attention to the day-to-day dips and surges in the market, and in the meantime we ignore these well-documented trends—trends that will unquestionably change lives, economies, and governments around the world. Global warming, for instance, receives a great deal of attention in the media, despite the continuing debate about whether or not it is actually occurring, and to what extent. Even the direst predictions of climatologists, however, pale in comparison to the impact global population trends will soon have on the globe. Terrorism, too, is frequently on our minds, even though years have passed since a major attack on U.S. soil. In the case of terrorism and global warming, of course, we would be wise to consider that there is much we do not know, to remain vigilant, and to continue to gather information. But while we do, the population time bomb is ticking, and there is *no doubt* that it will explode, almost before we know it. And that explosion will have profound repercussions on every continent and in every country on the planet.

To begin, let's take a look at present global population statistics by region,* data which will not surprise anyone who reads a newspaper or watches the news. Asia is now home to well over half of the world's population, with China and India alone accounting for more than 35 percent of the world's approximately 7 billion inhabitants. Africa is home to approximately 15 percent of the globe's residents, followed by Europe with 11 percent, Latin America with 9 percent, and North America with slightly more than 5 percent. Yes, that's right, the U.S. economy drives the global economy, and yet we need to add Canada's population to our own just to tip the scales at 5 percent of the world's inhabitants.

While the present population distribution falls into the category of things we *do know*, the rate of population growth, which will vary widely around the world, does not. And yet projections from a variety of sources are surprisingly consistent, and full of surprises. Who, for instance, is aware that while China's population is expected to rise to almost 1.5 billion by 2025, its population is expected to *decline* to approximately 1.4 billion by 2050? This is not true of India, whose present population of approximately 1.2 billion is expected to rise by 30 percent, to 1.6 billion, by 2050. Over the next 40 years the population of the Philippines is expected to rise even more rapidly—from 92 million to 146 million—and the population of Vietnam from 88 million to 112 million.

The real surprises, however—at least in terms of population growth—are Africa and Latin America. If the projections hold true,

---

* Most of this data can be found through the United Nations Department of Economic and Social Affairs Population Division.

the population of Eastern Africa will more than double in the next 40 years, from approximately 320 million to 710 million. The same astonishing rate of growth will occur in Western Africa, with the population there climbing from approximately 300 million to 625 million. In fact, gains will occur in every region of Africa—even in those areas hit hardest by HIV (primarily in Southern Africa)—more than doubling the continent's population to approximately 2 billion persons by 2050. Latin America and the Caribbean, while not coming close to Africa's phenomenal growth rate, are nonetheless expected to see their population rise from 580 million to 730 million in the next 40 years. Northern America's population, too, will experience steady growth, from approximately 350 million to 450 million—but that projection is highly dependent on continuing immigration. And yet despite that growth, given rising populations in other parts of the world, North America will still be home to only 5 percent of the *world's* population in 2050.

Equally surprising, and especially significant in terms of the world's economy, is the fact that population is actually falling in some regions. Both Japan and Korea will suffer serious declines in population, with the number of Japan's citizens falling from 127 million to 102 million by 2050. Every country in Eastern Europe is also expected to see noteworthy declines, with the region's total falling from 292 million to 240 million. Of particular importance, the population of the Russian Federation is expected to fall from 141 million to 116 million. And while Northern Europe's population is expected to grow slightly, Southern Europe will, at best, remain stable—at 150 million. Within that region however, Italy, Greece, and Portugal are expected to see significant declines. The same is true of Western Europe, where Germany alone will see its population fall from 82 million to 70 million.

One does not need a degree in economics to understand the effect such population declines will have on the global economy, especially in the case of the European Union, Japan, and Korea.

Equally important is the changing age distribution in the world's population. In its 2007 report on aging, the United Nations had this to say:

> Population aging is unprecedented, a process without parallel in the history of humanity. A population ages when increases in the proportion of older persons (that is, those aged 60 years or over) are accompanied by reductions in the proportion of children (persons under age 15) and then by declines in the proportions of persons in the working ages (15 to 59). At the world level, the number of older persons is expected to exceed the number of children for the first time in 2047. In the more developed regions, where population aging is far advanced, the number of children dropped below that of older persons in 1998.*

Yes, you read that correctly. The number of children in developed countries fell below the number of older persons *more than ten years ago.*

Over the next 40 years the number of those persons over 60 in Europe is projected to rise from 158 million to 236 million.† Nor will Asia be spared, where the number will rise from 399 million to more than 1.2 billion. During that time the number of Chinese over 60 will nearly triple, from 160 million to 440 million. And that sector of Africa's population will rise from 53 million to 212 mil-

---

* UN World Population on Aging, 2007.
† United Nations Population on Aging and Development, 2009.

lion. Europe will see a similarly steep increase, with its population of those over age 60 rising from 158 million to 236 million—and this in a region that will see a total population decline of almost 60 million persons in the next 40 years. Finally, while the number of those over 60 will rise across all of North America, in the United States alone the projected increase will almost double that group, from 56 million to 111 million.

Urbanization will accompany the changes cited above, with the following consequences.

> . . . world population will reach a landmark in 2008: for the first time in history the urban population will equal the rural popu-lation of the world, and from then on the majority of the world population will be urban. The world population is expected to be 70 percent urban in 2050.
>
> Between 2007 and 2050, the population living in urban areas is projected to gain 3.1 billion, passing from 3.3 billion in 2007 to 6.4 billion in 2050. *By midcentury the world's urban population will likely be the same size as the world's total population in 2004* [my italics].
>
> Furthermore, most of the population growth expected in urban areas will be concentrated in the cities and towns of the less devel-oped regions. Asia, in particular, is projected to see its urban population increase by 1.8 billion, Africa by 0.9 billion, and Latin America and the Caribbean by 0.2 billion. Population growth is therefore becoming largely an urban phenomenon concentrated in the developing world.*

---

* UN Urban and Rural Areas, 2007.

Lest you think this section has little to do with risk management, decision making, or investment strategies, reconsider the information above in the light of four different areas: economic politics, health care, taxes, and investment strategies.

The world's population shift toward Asia, Africa, and South America has profound political and economic implications. To begin, the populations of three of the world's five largest economies—the European Union, Japan, and Germany—will decline over the next 40 years, as will those of Italy, Russia, and South Korea. Those changes will unquestionably cause changes in global economic production, and will almost certainly tilt the balance of military power.

The effects of population aging will greatly exacerbate this trend, reducing the number of productive workers in the world's leading economies, while simultaneously causing the costs of health care to rise. In the United States the number of residents over the age of 60 will nearly double by 2050, from 56 million to 111 million, and thus a much smaller workforce will have to provide for a far larger number of retirees. Who among us believes that this alarming statistic will not affect Social Security benefits—and more importantly, payroll taxes—as well as the cost of government-sponsored health care? As for the costs of private health care—should it survive—it is worth noting that during the financial crisis of 2007–2009, as the number of jobs in the financial, manufacturing, construction, and service sectors fell like leaves in an autumn wind, the number of health-care jobs continued to rise.

Together these factors—shifts in demographics, economic production, and political power—will unquestionably alter the investment landscape for years to come. And while it's true that the numbers included above are all projections—and thus truly things we *do not know*—the trends are sufficiently alarming to warrant continual examination in the years to come.

To repeat, this is as good an example of something you don't know as you'll ever find, but perhaps knowing that you don't know, and knowing how important these trends will be over time, you'll keep an eye on them in the interest of de-risking your future.

A Story of Risk: Part 2

Rob was as comfortable in the world of private banking as a beach bum is in a hammock. He rarely got to work before 9:00, he took clients out to lunch almost every day, and he never missed the happy hour at his neighborhood bar. Sure, he had to do more than just sit behind his desk and answer the phone, but he had learned one or two things in school, the most important of which was that you should never do anything yourself before trying to find someone else to do it for you. He *was* good at bringing in new clients—many of whom were friends or acquaintances of his parents—but he left the numbers crunching to the guys in the back rooms. In fact, he was much more familiar with his commission and salary statements than he was with the bank's underlying business, or the nature of its portfolio. It was enough that the bank was paying him, and if the guys upstairs were making money too, that was just one more olive in the martini. Sure he heard people grumbling about interest rates, real estate values, and changes in the tax laws, but he preferred to look at the bright side.

Max had an entirely different view of the financial world, partly because of the two-part process followed by external auditors. Auditors first assess internal accounting controls to determine that the financial system is producing good numbers. Once satisfied that the process is in place, and that it's working, they test the numbers for reasonableness. How do they compare with last year's numbers? How do they compare to the industry as a whole? And pouring over the numbers of hundreds of smaller firms, Max saw signs of trouble.

His boss saw things a little more like Rob did. Yes, of course you had to come up with a statement, and if the numbers didn't balance you had no choice—unfortunately—but to bring it to someone's attention, but no one hired accountants to tell them their businesses were failing. Besides, a quick look at the most important numbers was usually enough. After all, you couldn't check every transaction. No, Max's boss preferred what he called the "fly-over" audit. All you had to do was to get into a helicopter at the end of the year and fly over each of the companies you audited. If their buildings were still standing, then who were you to tell them they aren't making money?

In other words, both Max's boss and Rob subscribed to the notion that what you don't know won't hurt you.

PART | 2

THE RULES OF
THE GAME

Risk Principle | 3

DETERMINE YOUR
APPETITE FOR RISK

*"And the day came when the risk it took to remain inside the bud
was more painful than the risk it took to blossom."*
—Anaïs Nin

Twins have been living in their mother's womb for nine months.
Their existence could not be more comfortable; all of their
physical needs are met. Then one day, they hear screams beyond
the uterine walls, and human voices. About that time the walls of
their living space begin to close in on them and one of the twins
descends—and then suddenly disappears. A moment later the
remaining twin hears a faint smack, and then the sound of his
former roommate crying. He reaches out into the darkness and
wonders what will happen to him. Will he too be forced out, or will
he remain where he is, comfortable but alone?

Of course our fictional fetus has very little choice in the matter,
although he doesn't know it yet. Either he will quickly leave of
his own free will—with a little maternal push, the first of many to

follow—or he'd better get ready to dodge the scalpel. Either way, for the rest of his life, he will never again be so comfortable. He will, however, have a lot more company, many more opportunities, and significantly more risk. And determining his appetite for the various risks that life involves—and offers—will affect his decision making for his entire life.

Every person's risk appetite—which, of course, varies throughout life—depends on a number of factors. Some of them are personal, some of them are social, and some of them are purely economic. Age is the most important of the personal factors. The young, as a rule, have both a greater appetite and a much higher tolerance for risk. The young, in fact, often seek danger for its own sake—perhaps because they have been shielded from it as children, and so want a look, or perhaps because they believe that any misfortune that befalls them can always be undone. They are also far more willing to risk both personal harm and the loss of their possessions because of their time-tested belief—confirmed by countless examples—that their families will come to their aid if things go wrong. Finally, the young are far less likely to have dependents, and thus if their fortunes change, or they suffer physical harm, they are able to convince themselves that they alone are affected. (A parent whose teenage daughter decides to drive home from college on an icy road has a different perspective, of course.)

Once one person settles in with another, however, their appetite for risk almost immediately declines. Add children, or adult dependents, and suddenly risk, once seductive, begins to lose its looks. It is one of the great ironies of life, however, that it is precisely at that moment that risk management becomes an even more essential component of one's life plan.

If your family depends on your income, what will happen if you are unable to work? Will your health insurance cover the *entire* cost of medical care if your husband or children become seriously ill? If your parents, or your spouse's parents, exhaust their resources, will you be able to care for them? Have you put money aside for your children's educations, and invested that money in such a way that it will, at the very least, keep pace with inflation? (Before you answer that question, I should make it clear that I'm not talking about garden-variety inflation here, the kind tracked by the Consumer Price Index, which consists of a weighted basket of goods and services, because it's a turtle compared to the hare of college tuition inflation. In the 20 years from 1978 to 2008 the CPI rose by a multiple of three—but college costs increased by a multiple of *ten*.)

The external factors that govern one's appetite for risk are innumerable, but primary among them is one's general sense of safety. Where instability reigns, and the events of the day can't be predicted with any certainty, risk is anathema. There is enough of it—in fact, there is too much of it—already present, and no sane person would attempt to add any more. Only in a stable social environment, therefore, does risk come into play.

One's appetite for risk is also clearly affected by personal circumstances—by wealth or poverty. Those without have little to lose, and so little to risk; those who possess more than enough to meet their basic needs can far more safely risk part of what they have. The ability to incur risk, however, does not always lead to the willingness to do so, a topic I'll turn to below.

While these basic factors all play their part to a greater or lesser degree, nearly everyone's risk appetite is determined by one essential calculation—that is, what do they have to do to *maintain* their current standard of living, or their present lifestyle? At first this may seem counterintuitive; one can easily understand why someone with great wealth would want to retain it, but why would someone with very little be equally satisfied with maintaining their circumstances? Many have written on this topic, but none more eloquently than the authors of the Declaration of Independence, who touched on this subject as part of their defense of the Colonial revolt.

> . . . all experience hath shewn that mankind are more disposed to suffer, while evils are sufferable, than to right themselves by abolishing the forms to which they are accustomed.

In other words, most of us would rather put up with the life we know than take a chance on change—a change which could, after all, leave us worse off than before. This bias has a great impact on our determination of risk appetite, but it is not the sole factor in our calculations. Our decisions are also influenced by a variety of purely human factors, most of which have existed for eons—that is, have been selected for over human history—but have only recently been included in the study of *how* we make decisions concerning risk. In this chapter I'll focus on four of these factors—loss aversion, risk aversion, probability and impact, and time frame. And since they also affect decision making, I'll return to them in later chapters.

Each of these, in its own way, relates to the determination of risk appetite in much the same way that the Efficient Market Hypothesis relates to actual market activities—in other words, the notion that we *rationally* determine risk is just as inaccurate as the theory that the markets are rational mechanisms, moving in response to prudent decisions made by investors on the basis of information available to all participants. If the events of the past decade have taught us anything, they have taught us that this simply isn't so.

To begin, *loss aversion* describes a basic human tendency already discussed above—the willingness to forgo an opportunity for gain rather than risking a loss, or the desire to accept what you have rather than reaching for more, and perhaps ending up worse off than you were to start. When applied to investing, loss aversion makes it *far less pleasant to make money than it is painful to lose it,* and as a result, most investors require a risk premium—that is, the chance to make more money than they risk losing—when faced with a choice involving potential losses. This seems to be especially true of those with considerable assets, whether individuals or institutions, and is reinforced by the Endowment Effect, or the tendency to attach a higher value to things we possess than the market does.

Risk aversion, instead, describes the preference most people have for certain smaller gains, even if by taking them they lose the *potential* for much larger gains. The appeal of a federally insured savings account with a low interest rate is a classic example, which many investors find preferable to investing in the stock markets, even though stocks present a far greater potential for gain. The flip side of the coin is equally mischievous. Given the choice between a certain but small loss, or the possibility of a far greater loss *or* a far greater gain, most people are inclined to accept the risk of a greater loss in order to have the chance at a greater gain. In other words, we have a natural—and somewhat irrational—tendency to accept small gains, and at the same time a willingness to risk losing a great deal more.

Again, circumstances and personal history either strengthen or curb these tendencies. I have often heard wealthy people from poor backgrounds make the following statement: "I grew up poor and there is no way I am going back." Young men, on the other hand, often tell you that their worst fear is having "to move back into their parent's house." Risk aversion, in other words, is highly personal. But no matter who you ask, most people have boundaries that they will not willingly cross. The important thing, therefore, is to know when you are crossing that line. It's not enough, in other words, to know your appetite for risk—when making decisions you also have to understand whether or not you have exceeded that appetite. And in that way you de-risk your decisions.

When I started my own hedge fund, for instance, I was very optimistic. My partner, however, although he shared my enthusiasm, always drew the line at certain personal liabilities. He was willing to risk his own money, in certain cases, but he always excluded his own real estate. Losing the roof over his head was a bright line he would not cross.

Probability and impact also affect our appetite for risk, where *probability* is the likelihood something will happen, and *impact* the effect it will have *should* it happen. This creates numerous opportunities for error—either when calculating probability, or when gauging impact—especially when you take into consideration the growing body of cognitive research that demonstrates just how difficult it is for the human brain to calculate probabilities. Perhaps the simplest example of this natural human deficiency occurs during a coin toss. Almost everyone believes, if two or three heads have come up in a row, that the odds have increased for tails. But this simply isn't so. Every time the coin is tossed there is an equal chance of heads or tails, and those odds *never* change. It is true that given a sufficient number of attempts, the heads and tails will eventually even out, but again, the probability of each individual toss never changes. (This tendency is exacerbated by our desire to see patterns, even where there are none, a topic I'll turn to when I discuss decision making.) Imagine, then, given how difficult it is for us to understand even the simplest probabilities, how little chance there is of us understanding the complex probabilities that exist in financial markets today. (This is also an excellent example of *knowing what we don't know.*)

Together, probability and impact create even greater mischief. If, for example, there is only a 1 percent probability of an event occurring—say the disappearance of a market for auction rate securities—an investment may appear to be safe. But if the impact to your portfolio—and more importantly, to the realization of your goals—is significant, then even 99–1 in your favor may be very poor odds. Auction rate securities did, in fact, prove to be an excellent example of our inability to correctly balance probability and impact. The upside in the case of auction rate securities—that is, the possibility of being paid a higher rate of interest, if the markets moved in that direction—proved to be far less valuable than the downside—that is, the impact on your portfolio should changes in the economy *completely close the market for such instruments*, forcing those who had invested in them to hold them until maturity. And this, as most of you know, is precisely what happened to individuals and institutions who bought such securities during the recent financial crisis.

Former Vice President Dick Cheney used a similar calculus to defend the Bush administration's anti-terrorism measures. For

Cheney, the impact of a nuclear or biological attack on a major U.S. city was sufficiently horrific that he supported what many have called draconian measures to prevent it from happening. For him, *any* probability such an event might occur was too high. Whether or not such a position is compatible with the principles of our Constitution is, of course, another topic altogether, and still hotly debated.

A story about author Lenore Skenazy, "America's Worst Mom" according to the Google rankings, further illustrates the point. Ms. Skenazy, after conferring with her husband, decided to let her nine-year-old son find his way home on a New York City subway. He had asked to be allowed to do this for years, and Skenazy finally consented, leaving him at Bloomingdales with $20, a Metro Pass card, and a handful of quarters in case he needed to make a phone call. (Curiously enough, she did not give him a cell phone, because she believed the risk was too great that he would lose it.)

In her book, *Free Range Kids*, Skenazy argues that we have lost our ability to assess risk—or perhaps better, to recognize risk. She put the odds of her son being kidnapped and killed by a stranger at about 1 in 1.5 million. Personally, I would reframe the answer by making it a question: Would you want to assume the risk of your child being kidnapped or killed even if the odds were 1 in 1.5 million? In other words, the probability of an event is meaningless if the impact, however unlikely, is intolerable. (This is also an example of framing bias, another topic to which I'll turn when discussing decision making.)

Probability and impact should also be considered when measuring *operational* risks, and these risks are usually mitigated by the use of what are called *challenge* controls. The need for such controls, however, depends on the probability of the event, and the impact should it occur. Suppose for example, a loss in an investor's portfolio is caused by an improperly executed trade. Once the investor has been made whole, management has to reevaluate the controls governing the firm's trades to determine if the impact is so large—for instance, the loss of investors' faith in the firm—that even the small probability of another, similar error cannot be risked. At that time management must also judge whether the proposed controls are truly sound—that is, will they effectively *eliminate* the probability of another such loss?

Finally, we also need to consider the *time frame* when judging our appetite for risk—that is, not only how long you can tolerate a specific risk, but at what cost. As well, you need to know how quickly you can reduce that risk if your appetite changes, or conditions turn against it. Suppose for example, you are trying to gauge the full impact of a power outage on your business—however small the probability may be that it will occur. If you can get your data center back online in one day instead of three, there's clearly a huge mitigation in cost. But what if the power loss is confined to your business? Then, because everyone else is up and running, even a 30-minute power outage will cost your business not only the money associated with operational losses, but may cost you clients as well. If that's the case, then you would be wise to install an emergency generator, as opposed to making arrangements with a third-party supplier for the use of their computer center during an outage.

Although it may not always be possible for us to overcome these biases, it is far more likely that we'll be able to accurately determine our appetite for risk if we understand that these biases exist; that they affect our decision making, and therefore our ability to de-risk our positions. The point is not only that our decisions are not necessarily rational, but that they are affected by completely unconnected events—a random number introduced before someone is asked to make a specific calculation—or by the way a question is framed.

Finally, there is the issue of peace of mind—which despite beliefs to the contrary, isn't necessarily associated with income. I once asked an exceptionally wealthy man, who had made his fortune underwriting penny stocks, whether he held onto stock from the companies he took public. He said he always sold the shares immediately after the initial offering, and invested the entire proceeds in Treasury bills. Didn't he believe the stocks he underwrote were good investments, I asked? He said he believed they were, or he wouldn't have put his good name behind them, but he suffered from extreme aversion to loss, and once the companies had gone public he could not accept the risk of their newly issued stock performing poorly. The downside of such poor performance would, to his way of thinking, be doubled for him. He would lose both his reputation for underwriting companies with hidden value, and he would lose his investment as well. Quite simply he was not comfortable living with both risks simultaneously. So converting his holdings to Treasury bills, even when those holdings were well positioned for gains, was necessary for his *peace of mind.*

One can also reframe this discussion in terms of comfort level, whether it involves the amount of money you have in the bank, the temperature in your house, or how long you are comfortable waiting at the airport—or in other words, the chance you're willing to take that you'll miss your flight. This is highly personal—not the sort of thing an investment advisor can, or should, dictate— but something we all know in our guts. We make these decisions every day of our lives, whether we're deciding how fast to drive on the highway, deciding how much cash to keep in our wallets, or deciding whether or not we should pull away from the curb before we see our children safely inside the house of a friend. Like the means necessary to maintain your lifestyle, or the conditions necessary to give you peace of mind, your innate sense of your level of comfort informs all your decisions regarding risk—whether you know it or not.

This brings to mind a risk management meeting I took part in years ago, when I worked for a large, well-known financial company. Along with the company's senior management I was asked to help make what we called a "how high is too high" decision. In other words, how much were we willing to lose in a given situation? We went around and around but finally settled on the following, simple answer—"too high" was a loss we would be embarrassed to read about on the front page of the *Wall Street Journal*. Staying below that number would give the company's management peace of mind. In other words, their appetite for risk depended on their tolerance for bad publicity. Accordingly, although no real financial principles were involved, we put limits on the company's portfolio so that its losses would never exceed the amount we could tolerate seeing on the front page of the newspaper.

One final example: Back in the 1990s Lloyds of London divided their custodial business between Chase Manhattan Bank and Citibank. Worried about nuclear war, Lloyds asked each bank whether their facilities could withstand a nuclear attack. Chase responded that not only would their vault withstand a nuclear attack, it would float even in the event that the island of Manhattan itself was destroyed. At Citibank, we looked at it differently. We told them that a bank vault the size of three football fields floating out to sea wouldn't be of much use to Lloyds, and that in the event of such an attack, both Lloyds and Citibank would have far bigger problems.

A Story of Risk: Part 3

By the late 1980s both Rob and Max were still living in the city, and although their apartments were only a 40-minute subway ride away from one another, they might just as well have been living in different states. It wasn't that they'd argued, or fallen out of touch. They still saw each other every other month or so, meeting up for a few drinks, or playing poker with old friends from school, but the lives they'd chosen kept their paths from crossing by chance. Partly that was because they had chosen different professions, but mostly it was because Max had married, and he and Barbara had two boys to raise.

Barbara, just like Max's mother, was happy at home—that is, as happy as a sleep-deprived young woman could be whose life revolved around the needs of her family. She and Max had finally found an apartment they both liked and could afford, in Park Slope, about 20 minutes from the Brooklyn Bridge. The neighborhood was still a little dangerous at night—which is why they could afford to buy the two-bedroom apartment—but it was changing fast, filling up with young married couples with children just like themselves. Nonetheless, Max had made it clear to Barbara that under no circumstances should she and the boys be out after dark.

He would have liked to spend more time with his family, but he had to be at his desk by 8:00 a.m., and often returned long after the boys, and sometimes even his wife, were already in bed. This was necessary because accounting was a volume trade—that is, earnings are calculated by multiplying hours times the billing rate—and both Max and his wife knew that his advancement depended on the number of hours he worked. Working toward a partnership, though, was a long-term plan, and so in the few free hours he had every week, Max continued to look for investment opportunities that might lead to more immediate gains—even at the risk of losing what he invested.

Max's father, a few months shy of 65, was still behind the wheel of a truck from 10 to 12 hours a day—that is, doing the same thing he had been doing since returning from the war 40 years earlier, with a medal on his chest, but no education or prospects. His three children were all out of the house now, married and working themselves; but as tired as the long years of work had left him, he knew no other way to go through the days. His wife still kept the apartment clean, did the shopping, and always had a hot meal on the table, no matter when he got home, but now that she was a grandmother, she took the bus from Brownsville to Park Slope at least three times a week, keeping an eye on the boys while Barbara did the laundry or the shopping.

Barbara's mother hadn't seen much of her grandchildren, because she spent her days taking care of Barbara's father, who had been diagnosed with early Alzheimer's. The emotional strain was considerable, and what was worse, their savings were gone. If not for her father's pension—he had worked for the city sanitation department—Barbara didn't know what her mother would do.

A world away, Rob still lived in the same building on the Upper East Side, but had all but given up hope of being able to buy an apartment in the City. Prices had gone through the roof during the early 1980s, and while his neighborhood was no longer as fashionable as it once was, his apartment was rent-controlled, and an easy subway ride from midtown, where the bank he worked for had its offices. His friends hadn't changed much either. In fact, to an outsider it may have seemed as if they were all still in college, with work taking the place of their classes, and their days just a prelude to their nights. The City was hopping, and they rented limos, ran up bar bills, and stumbled bleary-eyed past their doormen at 3:00 or 4:00 in the morning. Rob had had a couple serious girlfriends over the years, girls he met at or through work, but both of them tried to push the relationship to the next stage faster than he wanted, and so eventually they parted ways.

Rob's father had retired—or rather, had given up trying to *earn* money—and now spent his days reading investor's magazines, looking for one last chance at a big score; if he could just find the right start-up. His next door neighbor had sunk some money into a little computer company his son worked for, and never missed a chance to tell him how well the stock was doing when they talked across the hedges, but Rob's father was looking for something with more upside—an oil company, maybe, or a commercial real estate firm. One of his college roommates was making money hand over fist throwing up shopping malls in the Midwest, and when they saw each other at their 40th reunion had even offered him a chance to get in on the ground floor. The ground floor wasn't cheap, though, and if he was going to make it happen he'd have to convince his second wife to loosen the purse strings on the money she'd inherited when her mother died, something she'd shown no inclination to do up until then.

Max, in his own way, was doing the same thing. As hard as he worked he knew that there was no real future—that is, no big money—in accounting. It was just a way to pay the bills, and to put some money aside for starting a business, or investing. And that's how he got through the long days, knowing that his wife was keeping the home fires burning, and that he was slowly adding to his portfolio, which was heavy in high-risk stocks and contained no bonds whatsoever.

Risk Principle | 4

DEMAND TRANSPARENCY

"There are two ways of constructing a software design,
one way is to make it so simple that there are obviously
no deficiencies, and the other way is to make it
so complicated that there are no obvious deficiencies.
The first method is far more difficult."
—C.A.R. Hoare

Well over a hundred years ago, as part of a larger work, Mark Twain wrote the pages that have been removed intact as the short story "A Restless Night." The story concerns Twain and a traveling companion named Harris, who have taken a room in an inn, have put the lamps out, and have settled into their respective beds. Twain is unable to sleep. First he hears a mouse gnawing something in the dark, and after putting up with it for as long as he can, he takes a shoe from the floor by his bed and throws it toward the sound. The shoe hits the wall, and falls on Harris' head. Harris awakens briefly, and then goes back to sleep. Twain does not. Nor does the mouse. Twain throws a second shoe. It shatters a mirror.

Harris awakens again, but again is able to go back to sleep. Twain cannot.

Eventually he gives up any thought of sleep and decides to get dressed and go out into the square for a smoke. In the dark, however, he is unable to locate one of his socks, and gets down on his hands and knees to search for it. Making ever wider circles in the small room, he bumps up against chairs, sofas, tables, and umbrellas, making more noise than seems humanly possible. Finally, getting to his feet, he feels his way along one of the walls, and immediately knocks a large picture to the ground. Harris continues to sleep. Twain gets back on his hands and knees, now hoping only to find his bed again, and the jug of water next to it, because his efforts have made him thirsty. He finds nothing but more chairs, tables, and sofas, and so once again he gets to his feet in the dark. Finally, moving around the pitch-black room, he knocks a candlestick off the mantel, then nearly pushes a lamp off a table, and grabbing for it hits the water pitcher, which falls over onto Harris. This time Harris awakens, as does everyone else in the inn, including the owner. When he opens the door, lamp in hand, Twain is astonished to find himself in a small room with just one chair, one table, and one sofa. For more than an hour he had been going around in circles in the dark.

Complicated plans are oftentimes a sign of subterfuge, not sophistication. Put another way, thinking back to Twain's story, they are not the result of night's natural darkness, but of someone *intentionally* turning out the lights. If, for instance, someone tells you that the investment strategy they use is so complex that a simple explanation is beyond your understanding, your education, or your experience, it's almost second nature for us to concede the point.

After all, none of us knows everything, and besides, if we were to use investments as an example, the simple truth is that we *want* them to be handled by someone else, someone who knows more about them than we do, and it stands to reason that this sort of person would use a highly complex investment strategy.

But you might also quite reasonably ask yourself if there could be *another* reason that explains the speaker's unwillingness—or inability—to drag their methods out into the bright light of the day. Maybe, just maybe, those methods are left in the dark because they wouldn't withstand scrutiny. Finally, you might also ask yourself why you have decided to invest in a product, a vehicle, or a system you do not understand, managed by a person who is either unable or *unwilling* to explain it to you.

And yet this is exactly the way most of us approach certain kinds of decision making; we don't know what we're doing, so we pay someone else to make our decisions for us. And we often do so after little research or investigation—or what is commonly referred to as "due diligence." Instead, we tend to be swayed by good salesmanship.

Hype is everywhere. We live in a world transformed by almost unimaginable advances in communication, and as a result, a world that is blanketed with hype. And in the same way we accept—or even approve of—methods we can't understand, we embrace the hype. Who wants to take investment advice from someone who promises a steady 9 percent return—and over the *long term*? Or someone who insists that you include cost controls in your strategy, instead of just promising asset appreciation? That kind of advice just won't turn heads during cocktail party conversation, and let's face it—the investment stories one usually overhears are designed to impress those within earshot. By that logic, 25 percent annual returns, even if the speaker has no idea how those returns were achieved, will trump a story of steady, boring earnings every time.

The technology sector was hyped in this way during the 1990s. To understand the world of information technology, we were told, you needed a new paradigm. One for which the old rules were inapplicable. Old rules like turning a profit; or old business plans that didn't project annual growth of 25 percent—forever.

We all know what happened. The dotcom sector crashed and burned, and yet before the smoke stopped rising from the twisted wreckage of the new paradigm, the traveling hype show had already pitched their tents in front of real estate. All you had to do was to take advantage of low interest rates, courtesy of our good friends down at the Federal Reserve. It didn't matter whether you could afford a house or not—in fact, the way prices were going up, you couldn't afford *not* to buy one. And if for some reason you ever ran into trouble making the mortgage payment, all you had to do was sell your house—at a profit, of course—and move on.

Using that model of real estate investment it made sense to buy a house without putting a dime down on it. Who needed home equity when prices always went up? And why bother with a traditional mortgage when you could buy a house with an interest-only loan—at least for the first three years. Sure, you'd have a balloon payment to make in 36 months, but by then your house would be worth more money, because for more than 50 years real estate prices had never fallen. At least not for long. It's true, there had been a little dip in prices years earlier, and it had something to do with the Savings & Loan Crisis, but who could remember the details? After all, it happened sometime back in the financial Stone Age—that is, in the 1980s, before the new paradigm, before nothing-down mortgages, before adjustable-rate mortgages, before interest-only mortgages. And while it was true that if mortgage rates were already at all-time lows, the only direction for your mortgage to adjust was up; if you couldn't make the payments you could always sell your house, because prices just kept going up. And they always would.

And in the meantime, if you needed a little more cash to pay for a vacation, or another car, or college tuition for your kids, why not take out a home equity loan? Even if your "equity" was based on paper gains in the real estate market, not on the money you'd put down, or that part of the mortgage you'd eliminated by paying your bills. In other words, home buyers stopped thinking about houses as long-term investments, for which you had to pay, and began to think of them as a way to achieve a lifestyle beyond their means—like lottery tickets. It worked for a while—in fact, it worked for years—but it was a strategy based on the faulty assumption that *real estate prices would never fall*. And when they did, those who had decided to play the game, or had been enticed into playing the game, had bought into it so completely that they were flabbergasted when the house of cards collapsed. Afterward, in the space of just a few months, not only did they lose the paper equity they'd borrowed against, but faced the loss of their houses as well, which were no longer worth the money they'd agreed to pay for them. This model of home-buying simply wasn't transparent—or if it was, those who adopted it refused to consider the way it worked, and what might happen one day if it didn't.

During the period of rapidly rising housing prices mortgage originators, government agencies, and investment banks played a variation of the same game. Why worry about the underlying cash flows of the MBS and CDO they underwrote and held, even if those cash flows were the very thing that made the investments viable? Why indeed, when the majority of those mortgages ended up in the hands of Fannie Mae or Freddie Mac, and therefore were backed by the power of the U.S. government—even if the administration and members of Congress didn't come right out and say so. And not only that, as the debt piled up year after year certain members of Congress insisted that Fannie Mae and Freddie Mac buy even *more* mortgages, involving ever higher amounts of money. Everyone ought to be able to own their own home, after all—wasn't that the American way?

We all know what happened. Supply finally overwhelmed demand, and as prices stabilized, and then began to fall, foreclosures mounted, and the housing bubble burst. And once that happened the economy slowed, jobs disappeared, and in the space of a single-year retirement accounts, college accounts, and trust funds gave up ten years of gains.

Of course it's relatively easy to see the housing bubble for what it was now—that is, in retrospect. The job is far harder, though, as events unfold, but it is not impossible. Not if you insist on transparency from those with whom you do business, and demand a continuing, open dialogue regarding goals and risk appetite. Even when—or perhaps especially when—it seems the tide of hype has swept everyone else along. A healthy dose of cynicism doesn't hurt either. When something seems too good to be true—like steady, guaranteed returns, no matter what happens in the markets—it usually *isn't* true.

Which brings us to the well-publicized case of Bernie Madoff. Even a casual examination of his operation, based on simple, commonsense assessments, would have prevented investors from confusing its all too steady returns with sound investment fundamentals.

I speak from experience, having managed a fund of hedge funds, and having been responsible myself for the due diligence on many of the funds we selected. While funds of hedge funds are generally inefficient vehicles—because they involve fees both for the fund-of-fund management and for the management of the underlying funds themselves—they also provide investors with some diversification among hedge funds, as well as access to hedge funds with larger minimums, and most importantly, the institutional expertise necessary to conduct due diligence on the underlying funds. In other words, a fund of hedge funds is an easy but costly means of tapping the outsized returns of hedge funds, while enjoying a higher level of security, thanks to the due diligence of the fund of funds managers. This is not to say that investing in funds of funds absolves individual investors from their responsibilities. No matter how your money is invested, or by whom, you still have to demand thorough, transparent explanations of how and where your money is being put to work.

During that same period of my career the investment decisions of the fund I managed were handled by a single individual. Ordinarily, I would not recommend such a fund because I don't believe in one-man shows. If, to consider the worst case scenario, the manager got hit by a car, the fund would be in serious trouble. One-man shows, in other words, raise reasonable questions about conflicts of interest, segregation of duties, and business continuity. Nonetheless, in spite of those important concerns, I made an exception in the case of my fund *because of the fund's complete transparency.* As a manager I was provided with closing statements within an hour after trading, all pricing was done by an independent prime broker, full reconciliations between the fund and the prime broker were always available, the manager's performance reports were always timely and informative, and the manager himself had the majority of his net worth invested alongside other investors in the fund. In other words, I, just like every investor in the fund, could depend on complete transparency. Without it you have little chance of de-risking your investments.

A particularly instructive example of a highly sophisticated investor at first failing to follow these rules, and then correcting his error, involved the CEO of a renowned hedge fund. A mathematician by trade, as well as one of the world's most successful hedge fund managers—and a philanthropist of astounding generosity—he had been particularly supportive of one state university, and had donated tens of millions of dollars to the university's departments of mathematics and physics. The hedge fund manager also sat on the board at the university, and early in his tenure he encouraged the university to invest with Madoff. Shortly into the new century, however, the philanthropist's own hedge fund developed independent evidence that Madoff's business practices were suspect. In particular, his staff thought that Madoff's operation was not *sufficiently transparent.* As a result, the hedge fund manager tried to convince the board to pull the university's money out of Madoff's fund. Other members of the board disagreed, however, and while the endowment fund reduced its exposure, it eventually lost more than $5 million when Madoff's scheme was exposed. (It is especially interesting to note that when members of the investment committee pressed Madoff for details of his operation he refused to provide them, saying that he couldn't reveal his methods *because the hedge fund manager on the board was a competitor.*)

Again, insisting on transparency was all that was required to uncover Madoff's fraud. It was all that was necessary to de-risk the university's investment.

Below you'll find a relatively simple list of the questions I always asked before my fund invested in any other funds. By "simple" I mean that they are useful even if you don't have a graduate degree in mathematics, and not only that, reveal a great deal about any company, whether or not all the questions can be answered. Even a single red flag made me think twice. (These questions, of course, can be applied to almost any investment.)

1. Is there a free flow of information? How often, for instance is the fund's Net Asset Value (NAV) reported? Mutual funds report this number at the end of every trading day, and investors can find it in the newspaper or online. A good hedge fund will report its NAV at least once a month. Quarterly reports are important as well. If any of these reports are late, a savvy investor will ask why.

2. Does the hedge fund have premier suppliers? These suppliers include: the fund's prime broker (the firm that conducts its transactions and provides leverage); the fund's custodian (the firm that actually holds its assets); the fund's accounting firm; and the fund's legal firm. Are they all upper-tier, reputable suppliers?

3. Does the fund have the ability to stay in the game? New hedge fund managers may not raise money as quickly as they'd

hoped, or may adopt initial strategies that quickly bring the fund down because of a lack of capital.

4. Does the fund have a loyal investor base, and will its investors remain loyal when the going gets rough (because it always does, sooner or later)? Look for sophisticated investors with significant assets; if the fund's assets under management are made up of new, hot money, and the fund has no lockup provisions—that is, specific conditions under which assets can be redeemed—you should be worried.

5. Does the fund depend on a single stock picker, or is its success based on company-wide competence? Does the fund do its own research, or depend on numbers supplied to it?

6. Does the fund have a consistent approach? A good fund is focused, and doesn't adopt a new investment approach every other week. Does the fund have a track record of at least three years? It takes time to get a style down and build a good staff, and investors should be wary of startups.

7. Does the fund have an exploitable niche, and if so, is that niche sustainable?

8. Where is the firm in its growth cycle? Most good funds start with an incubation period, followed by rapid returns, and then a leveling off. Look for a fund on the upswing. If you invest in a fund at the top of its arc, you've got to wonder whether the managers still have the same fire in their bellies they once did—before they made the big money.

9. Does the fund's management have a good pedigree? Good fund managers come out of proprietary trading shops, where they learn how it's done, and just as importantly, how to put controls in place.

10. How large are the fund's assets under management? Look for a fund with AUM that aren't too small—indicating a lack of confidence—and not too big—which could lead to problems, depending on the investment style. And if the AUM is on the low side, can the management handle a suddenly increased asset inflow?

11. Do the fund's managers have skin in the game? Put another way, do the fund's managers eat their own cooking? If you feel pain, the fund's managers should feel pain too.

12. Does the fund's office space demonstrate a long-term commitment to the business?

13. Do the fund managers have transparent, easily monitored control functions in place (i.e., compliance, audit, risk management, etc.)? Is risk management embedded in the firm, and not just a police force working on the perimeter?

14. Are all of the fund managers and all of the fund's employees accessible? If you can't get to them, there's a good reason—that's bad for you.

15. Does the fund have succession and business continuity planning in place? It's one thing if power goes out to the whole city, and everybody's down, and another entirely if only the offices of that particular fund lose power, their servers go down, or they don't have multiple secure backups for their data.

16. Last but not least, does the fund's investment strategy *make sense*? In addition, are its returns reasonable given the historical returns in that specific market environment?

You may have noticed that I have not yet mentioned integrity or reputation, and by leaving them for last I have in some sense put the cart before the horse. An investigation of both are critical prerequisites to de-risking your investments. Sensibly included as a part of any due diligence, checking them involves investigating the managers' reputation in the marketplace, references from clients, and a search on past and current litigation. This is not to say that a fund's clientele is necessarily a good judge of management's character, especially if you ask them what they think during a bull market. But even during periods of high returns one can learn a great deal from what clients don't say. (Does management, for instance, frequently remind its clients that sound long-term investing involves losses as well as gains?)

Other factors also augur well for a fund's future. First among these is risk versus return. In other words, how much risk does a fund take in order to generate its returns? Yes, there are a variety of quantitative measures to get at this, but few of us have the expertise to interpret the data. Therefore, while not dismissing quantitative measures, I prefer to begin with another list of simple questions:

1. How concentrated are the fund's positions?
2. Does the fund's approach differ from the consensus of its particular market sector, and if so why, and how?
3. How much leverage is involved (i.e., how much money does the firm borrow to increase the amount, but not the percentage, of return on their investments)?
4. Are there any lockup provisions—that is, prohibitions on withdrawals?
5. Does the firm have guaranteed lines of credit?

As you will already have guessed, had you followed this simple list of due diligence fundamentals you wouldn't have looked twice at investing with Bernie Madoff. Yes, his reputation was excellent: He had even served as Chairman of the Board of Directors of the National Association of Securities Dealers (NASD). He was also an active philanthropist.

From the moment you began to examine his service suppliers, however, red flags would have begun to wave. His auditor had no other major clients, and worked out of a small office far from Wall Street. Nor did Madoff Investment Securities use the services of a prime broker—that is, a firm that executes trades, independently reports results, handles shareholder recordkeeping, and keeps records of asset valuations. As for the rest of the questions listed above, few asked them, and those who did never succeeded in getting any answers. The secrecy of Madoff's firm, in fact, and the inaccessibility of the man himself, actually helped create the mystique that led to the success of the swindle—at least in the short term. Seeing Mr. Madoff was all but impossible, as was knowing exactly how he made his investors money. (Pay no attention to the man behind the curtain.) If you were lucky, and knew the right people, Madoff might *allow* you to invest with him.

I had worked at Citibank for more than 20 years when I decided to open my own hedge fund. I put a presentation deck together and went out calling on high–net worth individuals to raise money. One of the first was a close acquaintance, a billionaire who sat through my presentation with attention and interest. But after 30 minutes he said: "David, there is no doubt in my mind you can do this, but I wouldn't invest a nickel in your fund until you quit your job at Citibank, spend at least $75,000 with a top-tier law firm to put together the necessary documents, and lastly, spend an entire year raising money, without any income. You have the experience and the understanding, but only if you did those last few things would I be convinced that you had the fire in your belly necessary to get this done." Substance alone was not enough for this man, who had an exceptional record as a long-term investor. Evidence of personal commitment on the part of management was a necessity for him—or in other words, another means of de-risking his investments.

The *lack* of commitment to certain ideals or standards will often lead to the same result. Many years ago, for instance, I served on the investment advisory committee of a charitable foundation. During my tenure the Chair of the Investment Committee had a major disagreement with the fund's Executive Director. The Investment Chair wanted the board to pass a resolution stipulating that the Executive Director could not spend *more than the investment income* of the endowment. In this way the endowment would not be depleted over time, and the foundation would continue to do its good work. The Executive Director won the argument—by firing everyone on the Investment Committee. He then turned the management of the endowment over to one of Madoff's feeder firms. Why? Because the Executive Director depended only on the firm's reputation, and didn't undertake even a minimum of due diligence, trusting instead the recommendations of a few Board members. He had stifled dissent, and rashly committed the foundation's future to a firm about which he knew almost nothing. The rest, just like the charity itself, is history.

A Story of Risk: Part 4

Max got to the poker game at Rob's apartment hours after the game had started, and listening to Rob and his friends, most of them bankers, talk about their plans for the weekend made him wonder if earning his CPA had been such a good idea after all. They were all sitting there in polo shirts and jeans, looking as if they didn't have a care in the world, while Max was still in a sweat-stained shirt and his suit pants. To hear them tell it, none of them ever showed up at work before 10:00 a.m., took long lunches with their "clients," and always got out of the office in time for happy hour. Not only that, they all seemed to be making as much money as he was—or at least it looked that way. Of course that could have been because he was the only one at the table who was married, and had four mouths to feed now instead of one.

There actually was one other married guy—Bill, a stock broker for one of the big brokerage firms—who played every once in a while, but he wasn't there that night. When Max asked about him they all looked at each other, but no one had much to say, other than he wasn't going to show that night. After another couple hands Rob told him they probably wouldn't be seeing Bill again, and then told Max why.

Bill had left his job at the brokerage about six months earlier. He'd never really been happy there, partly because he didn't like his bosses, and partly because he didn't like the business. Everyone talked about putting the customer first, but the truth was that every-one was pressured to steer their customers toward products that made the company more money. It wasn't really unethical, but the design of their clients' portfolios had as much to do with what was good for the company as it did what was good for the customer, and after five years of it Bill had had enough.

"What's the matter with that," asked one of the guys at the table, dropping his cards face down on the table. "You gotta pay the rent, don't you?"

Rob shrugged, checked his cards, called the bet, and went back to the story.

It turned out that Bill didn't just quit his job. He'd been looking for something else for months, and he finally found a guy somewhere down on Broadway who ran his own shop. Real nice place, to hear him talk about it. Mahogany paneling, crystal chandeliers, the whole nine yards. The guy worked only with high–net worth individuals. No institutions. Anyway, the catch was that the guy only took on people who could bring customers with them, which put Bill in a spot, since he had signed a "do not compete" agreement with his old firm. He worried about it at first, but finally decided that they'd never come after him, and so he went to his family and friends, rounded up a small group of investors—assuring them that he would personally handle their accounts—and jumped ship.

Bill's father, the largest investor of the group, had been a pretty well-known pediatric surgeon, but in his 50s he developed Parkinson's disease and had to quit practicing. He still lectured at the university, and did diagnostic work, but his hands had failed him, and his big money days were over. He was pretty well off by then, and put $500,000 of his money in his son's hands, asking only that the money be invested conservatively.

Anyway, Rob had run into Bill a couple months after he started the new job, and everything seemed to be going really well. In fact, he told Rob that if he had any sense he should think about opening up an account there, too. The guy who ran the place was a financial genius. Truly unbelievable. He did all his own research, handled all the transactions himself, and generated weekly statements for every single customer. And he never got in his brokers' way. He'd make suggestions, but everyone there was encouraged to make their own decisions. The only thing he pressed them on was bringing in new customers, but he made that easy, too. He had seats ten rows off the floor in the center aisle at the Garden; season tickets at Yankee Stadium, right in front of first base; and was on a first-name basis with all the maitre Ds at every good restaurant in town.

By that point in the story everyone had stopped playing cards. Max looked across the table at Rob.

"This story doesn't have a happy ending, does it?"

"Nope," said Rob, "it doesn't."

When Bill showed up for work a couple weeks back, the doors were padlocked. The Feds had closed the place down. He couldn't even get back in to get his personal stuff. His boss, the financial genius, the guy with all the tickets, and all the connections, and the best tables in the best restaurants, had been taking the money in through the front door and out through the back door the whole time. The weekly reports were just a cover.

"How much of his father's money did Bill lose?"

"All of it."

"Where is he now?"

"No one knows. His wife called me last night. She hasn't seen him for two days."

"All right," said the guy to Max's right, starting to shuffle the cards. "Enough of the sob stories. I'm down 50 bucks. Whose deal is it?"

Risk Principle | 5

DIVERSIFY

"You can get more with a kind word and a gun
than you can with a kind word alone."
—Al Capone

The great forests of the world are stunning examples of biological diversity. While distinguished by their largest life form, the trees that define them, those towering organisms are but the sentinels of the incredibly diverse range of life that exists beneath them. Plants, animals, and organisms too numerous to count live in their shade or mottled sunlight, feeding off the fruit, nuts, and organic matter the trees shed on the forest floor. And while from afar the forest appears monolithic, in fact it contains a wealth of individual habitats, each defined by the amount of sunlight it receives, by soil conditions and moisture, and demarcated by the biological needs of the flora and fauna that populate it. In normal conditions, these individual species move through their life cycles with little variation—when fire breaks out, however, their responses and their defense mechanisms are wildly dissimilar. Furthermore, those responses are dependent on the intensity, size, and duration of the fire, and on the frequency with which fire breaks out. As well, forest fires themselves are affected by seasonal changes and climatic conditions which can limit either their ability to ignite or to burn freely. Finally, while short-term conditions can reduce the possibility of fire—think of brush cleared by grazing animals, or periods of frequent rain—the longer the period between fires, the more intense the blaze when it finally breaks out.

The defense mechanisms of specific trees and plants, having evolved over unimaginably long periods of time, differ greatly. Some trees are able to resist frequent but low-intensity fires. Others, their leaves, branches, and trunks charred, have root systems that quickly throw up new shoots. Some, like conifers, have developed mechanisms to protect their seeds—for instance, pine cones that are actually activated by fire, opening and dropping their seeds only in extreme conditions. Some plants employ the same mechanism, actually increasing their range after fires. Other plants thrive in the moist, well-shaded conditions least likely to be affected by fire. If, however, those conditions change—say, due to an extended drought—and fire strikes, they are defenseless.

Animals, instead, survive by escaping fire. Birds fly away, and deer run from the flames. Speed is their defense. Some of those with more limited mobility perish. But turtles take to the water, and burrowing animals seek the cool safety of the earth.

And once the fire has burned out the forest, its inhabitants must react to the changed conditions. Herd animals that lose their source of food attempt to establish new ranges, but their new environments may be unable to support an enlarged population. Predators who survive the fire, and find that their source of food has vanished, will also attempt to acquire new territory, but they too will encounter competition from other predators. Birds that nest in tall trees will be forced to find new homes. Fire-resistant plants, instead, will take advantage of the scorched soil to spread into areas other plants could not defend, while the seeds of fallen pines will grow quickly in the sunlight that the trees from which they dropped no longer block.

Diversity, in short, does not preserve the forest as it was before the fire. Some species die, and some flee, never to return. But the sheer diversity of life forms ensures that some species will survive disaster, and in some cases even flourish.

Returning to the quote from Al Capone above, kind words and guns may not be the first things that come to mind when investors think of diversification, but in theory that combination of communication skills and weaponry works much the same way a mixture of stocks, bonds, and cash does in a well-diversified portfolio. If you can't convince someone with a well-expressed pleasantry, then you can always appeal to their fear of death.

To the average investor, diversification means dividing their assets among various investment classes. If those asset classes have what is known as "negative correlation"—that is, an upward movement in one is matched by a downward movement in another—then the risk of a single market event that causes all assets to lose value simultaneously is significantly reduced.* You might, using a ridiculously simple projection of seasonal demand, invest in both a swimsuit manufacturer and a snowplow manufacturer; the swimsuits will sell well during the summer, and snowplows will sell well during the winter. It's true, of course, that if you achieve a *perfectly* negative correlation among your investments, you will reduce both the risk

---

* The range of this measurement is negative one to positive one, where zero means no correlation, plus one means perfect correlation, and minus one means complete negative correlation.

of loss *and* the chance of meaningful gains. For this reason diversified asset groups are *weighted* according to an investor's goals, risk appetite, and current market conditions. Put as simply as possible, you can de-risk your portfolio by diversifying your assets.

A classic example of this sort of diversification is a portfolio *unequally* divided between stocks and bonds. Stocks generally involve a higher risk—because their value is dependent on a number of variables, including management performance and market conditions—and therefore, given that they carry a greater risk of loss, they offer the *possibility* of higher returns. Bonds, on the other hand, involve a lower risk; the question is not whether their value will rise significantly, but whether the performance of the company that issues the bond will allow it to make timely payments on its obligations. Therefore, absent the same elements of risk present in stocks they generate lower returns.

The recent financial crisis, however, in conjunction with a careful reexamination of past crises, show us that *correlation between asset classes rises fast when trouble occurs.* Greed may drive bull markets, but fear propels bear markets, and as that fear spreads, a rapid role reversal takes place: The bulls go into hibernation, and the bears stampede toward safety. The same research shows, however, that a sensibly diversified portfolio will not only survive a market crisis with smaller losses, but will recoup those losses more quickly.

The recent convulsions in the markets provide ample evidence of this pattern. After a five-year bull market that began in 2002—on the heels of the dotcom bust and the attack on the World Trade Centers—in 2007, the markets began to react to continuing devaluations in MBS driven by falling housing prices and mortgage defaults. This led to a reasonable concern on the part of investors that the fallout would affect not only the financial industry, but the U.S. economy as a whole. Despite efforts on the part of the federal government to allay investors' fears, which succeeded over the short term, the markets finally succumbed to mounting bad news, prompting the second most precipitous decline in the history of the Dow Jones Industrial Average.

While partly a result of highly leveraged positions, which magnified losses and led to margin calls that compelled both investment firms and individuals to cover their positions through forced sales—further depressing the values of noncash assets—the severity and the longevity of the downturn was primarily the result of an abrupt loss of confidence; or put another way, in a decline in the entire market's appetite for risk. And once the flight to safety began, it was as irresistible to most investors as the bull market that preceded it. As a result, even supposedly uncorrelated asset classes—like stocks, bonds, currencies, and commodities—experienced a simultaneous free-fall.

This rapid growth in correlation across supposedly diversified asset groups is in fact quite common during financial crises, owing to increased volatility. And that raises questions about the return investors need during crises to compensate them for increased risks.

The classic 60/40 allocation between equities and fixed-income investments provides a useful example, especially when considered in light of risk aversion—or the differing emotional responses an investor has to losses and gains. As I've pointed out earlier, investors are usually far more disturbed by losses than they are pleased by returns, and therefore as volatility climbs they need to reconsider their allocations in light of this psychological predisposition. If volatility doubles, for instance, as it often does during market turn-arounds, then investors need to ask themselves whether a doubled potential for gains adequately indemnifies them for a doubled risk of losses. And since this is not usually the case—because investors are more willing to accept smaller gains than to risk larger losses—then during periods of increased volatility investors need to recon-sider their allocations, accepting larger risks only if the potential for returns *far* outweighs the possibility of losses. And if that is not the case, then they should adjust their portfolios accordingly—that is, they should de-risk their investments.

Doing this in a timely manner, of course, depends both on inves-tors' awareness of volatility and their ability to measure it, and espe-cially on their ability to distinguish between short-term swings and long-term corrections. Historic data presents us with reasonably accurate long-term ranges of volatility—which we can use to judge current conditions—but keeping an eye on mid-term, and even short-term, volatility is just as important. In fact, once the direction of the economy begins to turn, investors should look toward short-term spikes in volatility as signs that the time has come to reevaluate their allocations—again, given their particular appetites for risk.

To understand this better it may be helpful to consider the rela-tionship between interest rates and global equities—or the prin-cipal sources of risk in most portfolios—and their correlation. In general, as interest rates rise equities suffer, and for a very simple reason. Why should you take the chance that GM will sell more cars, which will in turn push the price of their stock up, when you can get a reasonable return on bonds? Conversely, when interest rates are low, why bank your discretionary funds, since the markets offer a far greater chance for gains?

When inflation runs high, however, the correlation between stocks and interest rates tends to rise, as it did during the 1970s. In such an environment, the yield on bonds is quickly outstripped by the higher returns of other investment vehicles, and thus the price of bonds falls. At the same time the value of stocks, in order to be attractive, must first appreciate past the rate of inflation, and then provide *additional* return, and as inflation continues to rise and that sort of performance becomes less and less likely, investors flee from stocks too, pushing *their* prices lower.

During bear markets the correlation reverts to normal—that is, the correlation is negative. Stock prices are battered, and investors flee to the safety of fixed-income investments. And this negative correlation, if spotted before trouble begins, can work just as rising volatility does—that is, as a sign that you might reconsider your allocations before it is too late to de-risk them.

The examples above—that is, market crises, periods of high inflation, and bear markets—all occur outside "normal" market fluctuations (if such a term can be used). The value of diversification, however, is especially powerful over the long term, during both bull and bear markets, as well as through less volatile periods in the markets. To understand this it is important to look at the performance of diversified portfolios not only when they fail to protect investors from severe market shocks—which, as I've noted above, virtually no portfolio can withstand, unless it is accompanied by a crystal ball that can be used to successfully time the market—but also how such portfolios respond *once markets stabilize*. When that occurs—and generally speaking, the faster the crash the more quickly equilibrium is reached—broadly diversified portfolios immediately begin to prove their worth, because during the decline some asset groups are simply *victims* of the flight to safety, not underlying drivers of the instability that caused it. In 2008, for instance, as the equities markets continued to fall, the value of Treasury bonds rose, and in 2009, as bond prices stabilized, the equities markets surged. So, while these traditionally *uncorrelated* assets may have fallen together during the crisis, once an equilibrium of sorts was reached, they quickly parted ways.

In a portfolio made up of stocks and bonds, then, what constitutes optimal diversification? The answer depends on two factors: age, or investment time frame, and risk appetite.

Generally speaking, a younger person is in a far better position to benefit from higher risks simply because their time frame is longer. While the value of their investments will rise and fall over time, just as it will for older investors, they will have more time to recover losses—and even more importantly, their gains will be multiplied over the years because of the effect of compounding. Therefore, if the young invest in a disproportionately large share of equities, and enjoy early gains, those gains will be multiplied over the years that follow, compensating them for the additional risk. Conversely, as the time frame shrinks for older investors, the benefits of compounding are reduced. As a result, during the latter stages of life, and especially after retirement, you'll want to protect the money you've saved over your lifetime by shielding it from the short-term vagaries of the markets. Then, a steady stream of unearned income will be more important than the growth of capital, and as a result, your portfolio should be rebalanced toward more bonds, or fixed-income instruments, and fewer stocks.

This, of course, is just a general rule, and applying it blindly may cause as many problems as blithely ignoring it. The primary determinant of risk appetite, as we saw in Risk Principle 3, is lifestyle maintenance. In other words, both the rich and the poor would rather maintain what they have than risk a reduction in their standard of living. For a retiree, then, satisfying the needs of his or her core lifestyle is paramount, and only after those needs have been satisfied should emergency reserves, discretionary spending, legacies, and charity enter the planning picture. Cost control is also much more important in retirement, when it is no longer possible to work longer hours to cover rising costs. Inflation, too, is a critical factor. If a portfolio is heavily weighted toward bonds, it may still deliver reasonably high returns—say, between 2 and 4 percent—and yet lose buying power. Tax considerations are equally important, and the word "return" has little meaning *before* taxes are levied. So, while diversification will naturally lead investors to a larger proportion of fixed-income investments in retirement, the rule is not absolute.

As I pointed out earlier, there is a strong correlation between youth and the appetite for risk. But individual circumstances vary, and some older investors may still feel comfortable with a larger measure of risk, or even feel *compelled* to take on a larger amount of risk. That might happen because of unforeseeable losses in capital—a circumstance with which almost every investor in the past few years is painfully familiar—previously unanticipated needs, or new wants. The point is that diversification is not a one-size-fits-all model, but a valuable approach that will nonetheless change as age, needs, conditions, and wants change.

That lesson was driven home early in my career when I worked at Citicorp. At the time, Walter Wriston was Chairman of the Board. A giant in the world of commercial banking, and a man of considerable influence outside his own sphere, Wriston was eulogized by three former Secretaries of State at his funeral. About six months before he died, I ran into him, and after we'd exchanged the usual pleasantries he asked me: "So, how's risk management going David?" I responded: "Walt, risk is a four-letter word, but there's nothing wrong with using it as long as you can manage it." He smiled from ear to ear—after all, I was quoting the title of the book he wrote in 1987, *Risk and Other Four-Letter Words*. I not only read his book, but took its lessons to heart. Risk is not something to be avoided—it is an integral part of any successful decision-making strategy, as long as it's managed properly.

Many of the basic rules of diversification are indistinguishable from simple commonsense. Don't, for example, put all of your retirement money in the stock of the company you work for. (If you doubt the value of this advice, simply talk to anyone who worked for Lehman Brothers, Bear Stearns, or Enron—and *didn't* follow it.) If the company fails, you lose not only the source of your income, but also your retirement savings.

Similarly, don't keep your liquid assets—or cash—in just one bank. This exposes you to *concentration risk*. Because the FDIC protects only $250,000 of your savings in any one bank—the previous limit was $100,000, but was adjusted upward during the financial crisis—if your cash position exceeds that amount you should divide it between accounts in different banks so that *all* your money will be protected. Concentration risk, though, is not limited to cash, and can often work against you in unexpected ways.

Suppose, for instance, you are invested in a smaller hedge fund in which one investor owns 40 percent of the total assets under management. If she is able to exit her position—because the fund does not enforce lockup provisions—and she decides to do so for whatever reason, the manager of the fund will have no choice but to raise cash to satisfy her demands. Typically, this forces the fund manager to sell his most liquid positions, which may mean that the next investor who seeks to redeem his holdings may be unable to do so—at least not in the short term. The large investor's redemptions may also force the fund manager to liquidate some of his longer-term positions—whether or not they have had time to mature—and in so doing weaken the fund's core strategy. Concentration risk, then, whether in cash holdings or longer-term investments, can defeat diversification strategies.

To mitigate the danger of concentration, many institutional investors depend on an array of risk measurements. These include: Tracking Error, or the value of a certain position compared to a generally accepted benchmark; Value at Risk (VaR), or the maximum amount a position can lose in a given time period; and Beta, or the correlation of a position with the market. However valuable these comparisons may be in theory, in practice they are usually applied within, not across a portfolio, leading to a potential *overestimation* of the benefits of diversification when the same underlying factors affect supposedly different asset classes. Examples of this sort of *presumed* diversification include public and private equities, value and growth stocks, and the stocks of emerging and developed countries in the same portfolio. Again, one need only look back to the financial crisis of 2007 and 2008 to understand the dangers of such an approach. During those troubled times, all sectors plummeted simultaneously.

Time, generally a boon to the long-term investor, can work against you when you're pressed. The best time to look for a banker is when you don't need one. If you wait until you need a mortgage to find a bank, you're taking an unnecessary risk; the economic environment may have changed and the tide may now be against you, even if your credit is impeccable. Nor should you wait to start networking until you've been laid off and are looking for work. People tend to get comfortable, lulled into a false sense of security—but you should never stop looking for a job. Always network, always have your resume up to date, and always maintain a proactive approach to job hunting, because as long as you work, your job is part of your diversification strategy.

It is equally instructive to see how diversification works far outside the financial arena. Billy Beane, the longtime General Manager of the Oakland Athletics baseball team, manages his team by avoiding large payrolls—and the superstars who create them. Instead of relying on a handful of star players, as most other managers do, Billy hires players with specific skill sets. To do this he makes use of a relatively new method of analysis known as *sabermetrics*. (The word was coined from the acronym for the Society for American Baseball Research, or SABR.) In short, Beane uses sabermetrics to judge a player's ability to help his team win games, not individual batting titles or home run derbies. By this measure, a player's *on base percentage* is far more important than his *batting average*.

In other words, rather than depending on one or two high-cost investments—that is, superstars—Beane hedges his bets by taking *multiple risks*, or by diversifying the team's assets across the roster. Under his tenure this approach has not yet brought a World Series title to Oakland, but Beane's teams have had an exceptionally low cost per victory. Thus, even in the absence of the pennant, the team is profitable. His teams are also more likely to stay together, and to support each other, because each player knows the success of the team depends on *all* of them doing what they do best. A baseball superstar, on the other hand, knows that he can always take his personal skills to another team—and in fact may have to do that in order to maximize his salary. It's only fair to note, in concluding, that the Oakland As also benefit handsomely from the league's profit sharing rules, but that, too, is another measure of the success of Beane's approach.

Another way to diversify risk, especially for those who do not have multiple sources of income, is to have what I call an anchor. I use the word in the same sense a sailor does—an object, whether made of canvas or iron, that keeps your boat from drifting with the currents if your sails are torn, or your motor seizes up.

For most people, their primary anchor is their job. This is as true of high–net worth individuals as it is of those in the middle class, continually struggling to make ends meet. A steady stream of earned income, no matter your income tax bracket, makes diversification possible—that is, it allows you to separate your investment strategies from your monthly budget. If you lose your job, however, and don't have a cushion to carry you until you find another, you have lost not only your job, but a critical part of your diversification strategy. This is also true of the equity in your house—a classic anchor—especially when that equity has increased as the result of steady mortgage payments, instead of rising real estate prices, which as recent history has shown us, can be extremely short-lived.

Other anchors are psychological, and in the end may turn out not to be anchors at all. A close friend of mine, for example, was once a scientist at Xerox. There, he helped create the now famous Xerox Learning Center. After many years, he left Xerox and became a management consultant specializing in strategic planning. He very quickly began to "print" money with his new business, and one day I asked him why it took him so long to strike out on his own. He said that Xerox had a fabulous health plan, and because he had a family he was always afraid to give it up. It was a psychological anchor on which he depended. Once he left Xerox, however, he found he could buy the best medical plan on the market for only $1,500 a month (in those days)—or far, far less, on an annual basis, than the difference between his present and former income. In his mind, then, his medical plan was an anchor against life's physical uncertainties, but once he was out in the marketplace he found he could easily put that anchor down himself.

For those who are able—and I include both individuals and corporations—tucking away one to two years of operating expenses can also provide a suitable anchor during rough weather. Alan Mullaly's defensive borrowing as the CEO of Ford is an excellent example of this sort of anchor. When the credit markets seized up, he had already diversified the company's assets into a large cash position, and as a result, unlike GM and Chrysler, was able to continue doing business without driving to Washington, D.C., with his corporation's hat in his hand.

Harvard University's recent investment strategies were not executed with the same foresight, and, through their short-term failure, demonstrated the need for liquidity in a successful diversification strategy. During the financial boom of the first years of the twenty-first century, Harvard University's endowment fund, able to benefit from an unusually long-term investment perspective, incurred the risks associated with investing in highly illiquid assets—like timber and natural resources—in order to realize higher long-term gains. As a result, Harvard's operating budget, a portion of which was dependent on endowment returns, took a big hit after September 2008. When the value of their illiquid investments fell precipitously, they did not have an anchor to sustain their day-to-day expenditures. The point, once again, is that risk appetite, which drives asset allocations, and diversification, which spreads risk, are meaningless unless considered alongside an individual's or an institution's investment time frame. And if core "lifestyle" costs during that time frame aren't carefully enumerated, and anchors aren't put down to keep either the individual or institution from drifting with the economic currents, then true diversification doesn't exist—or put another way, you can't de-risk your investments.

To finish, a good friend of mine who runs a large, successful hedge fund once asked me *how* he should think about risk. I told him he should think of his entire portfolio as having a dollar bill's worth of risk, but that he should only use dimes and nickels to place his bets. Dime bets require well-understood return, based on volatility. With the nickels, one can be more adventurous. The trick involves not only knowing which investments merit dimes and which merit nickels, but more importantly, to remain faithful to your allocation plan once you've made your bets. So if a position works out well, and its appreciation takes it to a larger percentage of the total portfolio, it's time to start selling out of it. You can't argue with a gain, but the point is that if a position pays off—in essence, becoming a quarter—it's time to divide it into nickels and dimes again and reinvest them accordingly.

A Story of Risk: Part 5

As Max sat at his desk one day, working on an interim audit, he found himself thinking about a kid he knew in the old days, whose father had the best job imaginable. While Max's father went to work every day except Sunday, and put in long hours, his friend's father worked only *one day a week*, collecting coins from laundry machines in Brooklyn's housing projects. Every Sunday morning his friend's father would get into his truck and drive off, the local police would meet him at the door of the first Laundromat, and then lock him inside. He'd empty all the coins in the washers and dryers into a tool box and then the police would escort him back to his van. He spent the entire day doing the same thing, over and over again, Laundromat after Laundromat. By the time he got back home, his van would be full of tool boxes, heavy with coins, and Max's friend would help him carry them upstairs. On Monday, after school, Max's friend would count and roll the coins, using an old machine with a crank on the side, and then, every Tuesday, his friend's father would reload the rolled coins back into the tool boxes and drive to the bank. Once he'd made his deposit he would take the rest of the week off—that is, unless any of the laundry machines needed maintenance or repair.

Max was really impressed, and once he'd gotten to know his friend's father a little better he asked him how he'd been lucky enough to get the job. The man responded that it wasn't a matter of luck; he'd gotten the job by coming up with the right bid—that is, undercutting the price charged by the man who used to have the job—and that it had taken him years to figure out how to do it, and still make money on the job. The trick was simple, it turned out. You had to lose money on some of the Laundromats, and make it up on the others. And then hope no one bid on the job the following year, so you could push your prices back up.

Max's friend's father had started as a mechanic's apprentice, right out of high school, and had worked for years to get his master mechanic's license. Once he had it, though, he quickly realized that there was a limit to the amount of money he could make at his trade, and so he started thinking about what he could do to add to his income. In other words, earning his mechanic's license gave him an anchor, and that gave him the confidence he needed to take the additional risk of diversifying his income. After looking around for a year or so, he decided the Laundromat business was just what he was looking for, but it took him two or three years to come up with the winning bid. And by the way, Max had it all wrong. He didn't work only one day a week. He still worked as a mechanic, but now he could afford to take only the jobs he wanted, and so he was usually done by the time the boys got home from school. The point was that he had more than one source of income.

While Max was thinking about what he could do to add to his income, Rob was sitting in his boss's office. After a little small talk, his boss told him he'd singled Rob out for a special project.

The bank's upper-level management wanted someone to review the bank's commercial real estate portfolio, and since Rob had been hinting that he thought he was overdue for a promotion, this might be a way for him to make his case. Of course the report had to have his boss's name on it, but his boss would be happy to share the credit. It wasn't that tough a job anyway; it was just that his boss didn't have the time. Besides, the focus was relatively narrow. All management was concerned about was the size of the portfolio, given the gathering storm in the sector. There was just one more thing: The loans were heavy contributors to the bank's bottom line, so while Rob had to identify any trouble spots, a report suggesting that the bank should reduce their exposure to the sector probably wasn't what management wanted to hear.

Rob wasn't wild about the idea, but he was plenty smart enough to know that "yes" was the right answer. The problem was that he didn't know a lot about commercial real estate, although he had originated quite a few loans in the sector over the years. He was more of a rainmaker than a bean counter. So once he'd told his boss that he'd be happy to write the report, and had thanked him for the opportunity, he began to go through a mental list of his colleagues at the bank who might be able to help. By the time he got back to his office he thought he had just the man, and picked up the phone and called Stu Jones, an experienced, but past-his-prime banker. Would Stu like to join him for dinner the following night?

Over the course of dinner—at one of the city's premier steak houses, where the prices were sure to push Rob's American Express bill right up against the limits of his budget—Rob went to work picking his older colleague's brain. Stu, who had worked at the bank for more than 30 years, was touched that Rob had come to him for advice, and, well lubricated with scotch, he led Rob through the basics of commercial real estate analysis.

Like virtually every other bank in the business, theirs had a substantial commercial real estate portfolio. And while it was true, he said, that the sector was in trouble, and that things were likely to get worse before they got better, the bank's total portfolio was protected by two important factors. First, the loans were well diversified. They were spread out across the country, and therefore if one region suffered outsized losses, the other regions would provide support. Second, the majority of the loans had been made to premier developers, top-tier firms that had been in the business a long time, and knew what they were doing. The shakeout, which was real, might affect newcomers in the game, but the experienced developers knew how to get through a slump.

The next day Rob went to work. He gathered numbers to support his colleague's opinion, had his girlfriend, who worked for a publishing house, edit his draft, and the following Monday put a bound copy of the report on his boss's desk. His boss called him in later that morning, shook his hand, and congratulated him on a job well done, assuring him that his name would be mentioned when he made his presentation.

As luck would have it, his boss was as good as his word. He made the presentation, gave Rob a share of the credit, and management, satisfied that they were in better shape than most banks, even allowed their commercial real estate portfolio to grow a little more.

Within six months the entire sector crashed and burned. The wreckage littered the landscape of every region in the country, and took down the projects of developers large and small, including those new to the business as well as those with decades of experience. Management hadn't forgotten the names on the report, and both Rob and his boss were soon looking for jobs. Stu, much to his surprise, got a promotion. In fact, as one of the vice presidents showed Stu his new office, he told him that upper management could just kick themselves for not having asked *him* to review the commercial real estate portfolio himself, since he was an old hand in the business and would have seen the warning signs those two idiots hadn't.

Risk Principle | 6

CHECKS AND BALANCES

"The difference between fiction and reality?
Fiction has to make sense."
—Tom Clancy

Just like the natural diversification found in any forest, the effectiveness of which is revealed both during and after a fire, checks and balances exist in nature, too. What are our natural fears of darkness, heights, and sudden loud noises if not nature's way of checking dangerous behavior, or startling us into flight? And what is religion, present in every culture the world has known, but a human attempt to impose morality—that is, to check certain human behavior, and to promote personal and social balance? Justitia, the Roman Goddess of justice, holds a scale in one hand. She also wears a blindfold, to ensure impartiality, and holds a sword, to enforce her judgments. The Chinese philosophy of yin yang—or in the West, yin *and* yang—offers an ancient yet enduring concept of balance, and implicit in that philosophy is the belief that without yin, yang cannot exist. Our concept of heat, without the corresponding concept of cold, has no meaning. Light shines only in the darkness. We cannot soar to new heights if we cannot also fall to new lows.

Our habit, or one might say our need, to establish checks and balances extends to our most basic social conventions. What husband and wife, for instance, do not understand the concept of checks and balances—unless, perhaps, theirs is a wartime marriage, with the couple separated by an ocean, and all lines of communication shut off? Parents and children understand the idea all too well. Parents employ it daily, and children resist it from the moment they are able to walk.

Why then, with so many natural examples of checks and balances all around us, do we so often fail to implement them, or to check that they're in place before making decisions?

If risk management begins with determining where you are, and is followed by deciding where you want to go, then it naturally leads to determining the level of risk you'll accept to get there. None of these are easy things to do, nor are any of the decisions easy to make—and what's worse, you have to do them over and over again. Why? Because you'll find yourself in a different place every day of your life. You'll see greener grass every time you turn your head. And your appetite for risk may change as frequently as the weather.

The rest, fortunately, is somewhat more mechanical. Insist on transparency, so that you see your plans in action. Diversify, so that unforeseen fluctuations in the markets don't affect all your assets equally. And finally, establish checks and balances to confirm that your plans are being followed, and that your assets are safe.

The idea of checks and balances is hardly original, especially in the political realm. The ancient Greeks, and the Romans in their turn, divided their governments into three sections, each with its own authority and responsibilities. Over 200 years ago the idea resurfaced with the creation of the three separate branches of government in the United States—the Congress, the Executive Branch, and the Judiciary—in order to ensure the separation of political power, and the inability of any one of the branches to dominate the others. The founding fathers proposed this system in response to the theory of political power prevailing at the time—that is, that no matter who governed, on the basis of whatever authority, the thirst for power was insatiable, and it had to be checked. Madison, in the Federalist #51, began his appeal to the people of the state of New York, as they considered the ratification of the Constitution, with these words:

TO WHAT expedient, then, shall we finally resort, for maintaining in practice the necessary partition of power among the several departments, as laid down in the Constitution? The only answer that can be given is, that as all these exterior provisions [noted earlier] are found to be inadequate, the defect must be supplied, by so contriving the interior structure of the government as that its several constituent parts may, by their mutual relations, be the means of keeping each other in their proper places.

Given the results of the vote back in 1789, it appears the voting public of the day was able to find its way through that maze of words. And as a result, for more than two centuries the simple concept of the division of powers, in spite of war, economic turmoil, and frequent transfers of political power, has preserved our freedoms of speech, press, and assembly, and has ensured that no single branch of our government has been able to exceed its constitutional authority—at least not once the newspapers got wind of it.

Federalism is an example of checks and balances layered one on top of the other. The power of the federal government is distributed among three branches, but each of those have power only in the federal sphere—that is, in areas of government like civil liberties, national defense, environmental protection, and interstate commerce, which pertain to all the states. The states themselves, however, remain free to legislate matters of local taste—like tort law, building codes, and the nature of civil unions.

The applications are endless, but the procedure is simple: Make certain that there are controls in place that check—or you could say, challenge—the legitimacy of every transaction, and require every account to be balanced. Commonsense dictates that these functions be separated among institutions or persons. In other words, never let the person who balances your books manage your money, unless of course you do it yourself. If you doubt the wisdom of this strategy, perhaps the innumerable petitions filed in bankruptcy courts on behalf of musicians, actors, and professional athletes who have not will convince you of the danger. Do this *before* it's too late, and you have no chance to de-risk your business plans, because those petitions are usually filed long after the victims' accountants have cleaned out their bank accounts and then moved to foreign countries that have no extradition treaties with the United States. Again, checks and balances greatly reduce the risk that any one person, or institution, can grab the wheel out of your hands and take you off course—or slip a hand, unnoticed, into your pocket.

Checks and balances aren't useful only in financial matters— they can be applied to every aspect of your life, and to virtually every project you undertake. Project management, for instance, consists of a series of checks and balances. First the project is broken up into specific tasks, designed to produce specific deliverables. Someone is then made responsible for every deliverable, each with its own due date, and at that point the project manager need only monitor the deliverables.

If you're having your house remodeled, to use another example, you would be unwise to pay your contractor everything up front, thus depriving him of the single most powerful incentive he has to complete the job, as well as losing any bargaining power regarding the quality of his work, or its faithfulness to the blueprints. You'd do better—and so would he—if you and your contractor negotiated a system of checkpoints, so that when he completes one phase of the work (the plumbing, for instance), he gets a partial payment, and when he completes the next (for example, all the electrical work), he gets another payment. And once he has finished everything you hired him to do—including every last finishing touch—he gets his eagerly awaited, final 20 percent.

Of course, in order for a plan like this to work you have to make sure that it works for both you *and* your contractor—in other words, you'd do better to offer him a bonus, rather than a penalty, for the timely, satisfactory completion of the job. That way you can ensure that he'll do everything he's agreed to do—which will make *you* happy—in order to get his final bonus payment—which will make *him* happy. If, on the other hand, your contract includes a penalty in the event he doesn't finish the job, he may at some point make a decision that doesn't benefit either of you—that is, he may decide to walk away rather than finishing the job, because it's not worth it to him to complete it, given the penalty. But because people *hate* losing bonus money, you can minimize both your financial and your emotional risk by making it *worthwhile* for your contractor to finish the job to your satisfaction. (And as anyone who has ever hired someone to remodel their home knows, such projects are highly emotional.)

A more sophisticated financial example of this principle occurs when hedge fund managers reach what are known as "high water marks," which, after they've recouped any losses, allow them to withdraw their share of the profits they've made for their investors. In this way, investors believe that they can protect themselves by not allowing hedge fund operators to withdraw their share of the profits until the investors have first received *their* fair share. While this appears to be a sensible provision, consider the following: If a hedge fund manager loses enough money in any given year he or she may be faced with a situation in which they cannot possibly earn enough to reach their high water mark, thus making it impossible for them to be paid. Many investment managers faced with such a situation will wisely—at least in light of their own interests—refocus their attention on funds that may still allow them to make money, or worse yet, close down any fund likely to fall far short of its high water marks. The moral of this story—be careful what you ask for.

Checks and balances generally can be divided between those created by individuals, and those created by the institutions with which the individual investor does business. While these two sets of controls frequently overlap, the individual checks and balances depend on clear guidelines from the investor, as well as a complete understanding of the various risks involved with the active management of his portfolio. These include market risk, liquidity risk, leverage, and valuation. Institutional checks and balances, instead, depend on the variety and effectiveness of internal controls put into place—and monitored—by the investment firm itself. These include the assessment of operational risk, which is senior management's responsibility, and oversight mechanisms like independent controls, segregation of functions, and well-defined policies and procedures. They also include operational checks and balances—that is, transactions systems and business continuity. Individual investors cannot, of course, be expected to track the success of such institutional controls on a day-to-day basis, but without a basic understanding of such controls, an individual investor will not be able to conduct the due diligence necessary when choosing an investment firm.

Individual Checks and Balances

Turning first to individual checks and balances, clearly stated investment guidelines are the individual's first line of defense. While an investment advisor may assist a client in creating such guidelines, following the principles discussed earlier in this book—that is, knowing where you are, determining your appetite for risk, and diversifying your assets—will naturally lead each investor to create guidelines consistent with their investment goals. Almost all investment management firms have clear procedures for recognizing investors' guidelines, and for entering them into the record, but the specific mandates themselves are clearly the responsibility of the investor. In general, these will include the investor's risk tolerance, liquidity needs, and perhaps even specific requirements regarding allocation, but they may, for larger investors, also include the prohibition of certain equities, such as "sin" stocks—for example, tobacco, gaming, etc. Whatever their nature, each individual investor must make his or her desires known at the start, and must make sure that their directives are not only unambiguous, but do not require, or even allow the possibility of interpretation on the part of the investment firm. Furthermore, investors must make sure that the individual handling their assets is both capable of following the guidelines they have expressed and has the *authority* to do so. And while investment advisors cannot promise specific returns— and investors should be wary of those who do—investors should make their expectations regarding return clear as well. Usually this involves setting a range—say an annual return between 8 to 10 percent—and if those expectations are not met, or even if they are exceeded, the investor should know that they will hear from their advisor, and that previously outlined and well-understood procedures will be employed to attempt to bring their returns within their established guidelines. Investors must also continually balance their expectations for returns against the risk they have assumed to reach them. Management costs, too, are a part of this calculation, and may depend on the products or vehicles included in an investor's portfolio. Finally, the use of a defined benchmark, chosen because its management style and/or its portfolio parameters correspond to a specific investor's general guidelines, will help determine whether varying returns are the result of management decisions, or of the market in general. If an investor's portfolio is underperforming relative to its benchmark, a review should be made to determine the causes.

Another way to look at this involves setting investment "boundaries." These boundaries are first drawn by considering overall goals, and then by considering the objectives of each investment product in the portfolio. Each of these products should be discussed in terms of risk versus return, and together should fall within the investor's general risk tolerance. It may help to visualize these boundaries as being similar to the low walls that can be raised on either side of a lane in a bowling alley so that you can no longer throw a "gutter ball." The point is that the use of checks and balances all but force you to stay in the lane. You may not get a strike, but you'll always knock a few pins down, and in so doing de-risk your investments.

Monitoring performance, another critical part of checks and balances, is the job of both individual investors and institutions, and even after having been assured of the presence of institutional controls individuals must continue to check their portfolio's performance themselves, and to make sure that their advisors are doing so as well. Liquidity risk is another factor that both individuals and institutions must check continually.

Finally, as individual investor guidelines change, either in response to personal circumstances or market conditions, investors must communicate those changes to their advisors in a timely manner, making sure that the new guidelines have been officially recognized, and that their portfolio managers have reacted accordingly.

Institutional Checks and Balances

Institutional checks and balances, put in place both to help investors meet their goals, and to guard against undue organizational risks, can be grouped into two broad categories: governance and operations. Governance involves the development of checks and balances throughout the entire organization, and includes the segregation of front, middle, and back office functions,* the creation of a company-wide risk management culture, the existence of independent control groups, overall compliance, and the creation of explicit policies regarding personal authority and the ability to make exceptions to certain established procedures. Operational checks and balances cover the ordinary transactions of the business, including the organization's systems and procedures, and business continuity planning. Again, an individual investor cannot walk the hallways of her investment management firm every day, checking to be sure that everything is going according to her plan, but she can, by understanding the basics of governance and operational checks and balances, conduct due diligence before selecting an investment firm and then monitor the firm's performance once she has.

Governance

The segregation of front and back office functions ensures the independence of the various parts of the organization, or to put it another way, guards against conflicts of interest between those parts. Those persons responsible for bringing in new clients, for example, as well as those who manage existing accounts, should not be responsible for determining the creditworthiness of the firm's clients. Nor should those managing accounts be responsible for operational procedures—like settling trades or valuing trades—

---

* Front office functions include portfolio management and research and trading; middle office functions include customer support, new accounts, and recordkeeping; and back office functions include operations and systems management.

either when they are made or as they are valued over time. This prevents misstatements—whether intentional or as the result of simple human error—from going unnoticed. Nor should traders or managers be able to determine who and under what circumstance exceptions can be made to established procedures—for example, taking positions outside the client's guidelines, or outside those of the firm.

Senior management is responsible for a number of checks and balances, first among them the company's enterprise-wide risk management strategy, or the procedures that are used to identify risk, measure risk, and monitor and control risk, as well as the degree to which risk should be employed to meet the goals of the firm and its clients. A strict adherence to such checks and balances will greatly reduce the possibility of unanticipated losses, loss of confidence in the firm, operational disasters, or failures of compliance.

Senior management is also responsible for ensuring the independence of the various control groups checking and balancing risk. For that to happen, control groups should preferably report directly to senior management—if not to the board itself, or to the CEO—not to the business units they monitor. A Chief Risk Officer (CRO) can also be put into place to direct a variety of control functions and to propose enterprise-wide checks and balances, but will succeed only if such a person has a place at senior management's table, and a *voice* there as well. And while a CRO can also create specific, written policies and clearly stated institutional procedures far more effectively than a collection of control groups can, senior management might also decide to separate operational risk controls from strategic risk controls, or from portfolio risk controls, and might even choose to subcontract one or another of those services depending on the talents of the company's personnel, or the experience of senior management.

Stress testing both an organization's total portfolio, and investors' individual portfolios, is also an important part of checks and balances. This can be done quantitatively, using specific metrics and/or models from the top down, or it can be done from the bottom up—for example, by individual portfolio managers continually tracking interest rate shifts, changes in volatility, and credit spreads.

Checks and balances must also extend to the firm's fiduciary responsibilities, both to clients and to employees. Those responsibilities should be clearly stated in all legal documents, as well as any internal directives. Nor does a firm's fiduciary responsibility disappear if it places a client's assets with third parties—in effect, such a move simply creates another risk management responsibility.

Controls must also exist for compliance, which in its simplest form involves ensuring that your account, and the firm that manages it, is in compliance with the law. This means protecting clients from a series of proscribed behaviors, including front running (trading ahead of the client to take advantage of, or influence the price of, an asset), best execution (getting the best price when the trade is executed), and treating all clients fairly (not giving one client an advantage over another). Actions of this sort can clearly create conflicts of interest disadvantageous to certain investors, and yet such behavior is not prohibited in all markets.

In some countries, for example, it is permissible for an investment manager to own stock in companies in which he invests on behalf of his clients. One needn't be an experienced investor to understand the potential for conflicts of interest in such a situation.

There are many other examples that demonstrate just how closely compliance and risk are linked. If, for instance, a compliance officer finds that a portfolio has exceeded its allocation guidelines—say, an over-concentration in a particular class of stock—a correction is as important from a risk management perspective as much as it is from a compliance perspective.

Continuing along these lines, an internal audit may be considered as the last line of institutional defense. Internal audit's job is to dig deeply into the innermost workings of an investment company in order to ensure that all of its divisions—each with their own responsibilities—are functioning properly. One of the many benefits of successful internal audits is the knowledge that risk and compliance functions are both working properly, and in tandem.

Operations

Operational checks and balances exist to mitigate errors made in the ordinary course of business, as well as dangers to the organization's operational capabilities during disasters. The former group includes day-to-day errors, and the inevitable snafus that occur in complicated systems—as well as the age and health of those systems themselves. The attack on the World Trade Centers clearly falls into disaster preparation, as does the last major failure of the electrical grid along the Eastern Seaboard. In cases such as these, companies must not only have plans in place to deal with catastrophes, should they occur, but must also change their strategic planning to include the possibility of such calamities, and take steps *beforehand* to diminish the consequences.

For these checks and balances to succeed, the organization must first identify the elements of back office operations subject to such risks. This list generally includes those instances when a trade fails or there are reconciliation differences, customer service and customer complaints, guideline infractions, and a variety of systems issues. To effectively protect these vital systems, operations must be continually monitored, and recurring problems identified before they can assume dangerous proportions. And while manual processes are generally responsible for more errors than automated processes, the technology behind such automation is constantly advancing, and thus must be updated as frequently as possible, and replaced on a timely basis. This is especially true of the hi-tech tools used for bookkeeping and records storage, and risk management and compliance. End-user tools, like individual spreadsheets used by portfolio managers, can pose serious problems if they are not included in company-wide databases (where they can be accessed and checked by someone other than the end user). Again, an individual investor cannot monitor such controls at the investment firm with which he does business, but he can ensure that enterprise-wide operational checks and balances are utilized when he performs his due diligence—before committing his assets.

Models require the same sort of checks and balances. Whether used for official calculations—for instance, valuations, fee calculations, etc.—or for analytical purposes, they must be evaluated when they first come into use, over time, and whenever market conditions have changed since their last use. Specifically, both the data and the assumptions on which the models are based should be reviewed, the models' algorithms should be reexamined, the uses of the models should be reconsidered, and the impact of any weaknesses in the model should be stress-tested against historical data and volatility indices.

Adequate backup and recovery of data—either as a result of local problems, mechanical failures, or natural disasters—is another critical operational consideration. Offsite backups of both data *and* systems, spread out as widely as possible, and if possible, dependent on different power grids, are a critical component of disaster planning. Making certain that the institution with which you do business is not concentrated in one location is another. Again, think of those businesses whose entire operations were housed in one of the World Trade Centers.

Security, to conclude this section, is another vital consideration. Customer data and enterprise-wide databases must be secure not only from outside attack—that is, from hackers—but from viruses unintentionally released by employees, or simple human error. As the old saying goes, there are only two kinds of computer users—those who have lost data, and those who will. Physical security is an equally important concern, both for clients and employees of any investment firm. Again, individual investors won't want to set up a stake-out to evaluate their investment manager's security, but if you are able to walk past the front desk without being challenged, you might ask yourself who else can, why they might want to do it, and what the consequences might be.

Years ago, when I worked for John Reed, then CEO of Citibank, people from outside the firm would often ask me what I did for him. My answer was simple:

"Whatever he wants—quickly."

When Reed moved me into risk management, the staff there asked me the same question. To them I responded:

"I let him sleep better at night."

I think the same is true for compliance and internal audit functions—or, in other words, for the checks and balances that protect both the firm and its clients. While the spotlight may be on risk management, I think that in the future investment firms will have a new sort of CFO—that is, not a Chief Financial Officer, but a *Chief Fiduciary Officer*—one responsible for risk management, compliance, and internal audit. As a risk officer, he or she will make certain that the firm's clients are not exposed to undue risk, and as a compliance officer that the letter of the law, and the client's guidelines, are followed. Finally, as an internal auditor, the officer will ensure that all controls are working together to protect both clients and the firm itself.

To some extent, each individual investor should attempt to assume a similar function herself. The point is that one hand can't wash itself. With both involved, however—that is, with your oversight, and the internal controls of the firm with which you've entrusted your money—you can expect a reasonable level of cleanliness.

It is equally important, as I pointed out in Risk Principle 2, that investment firms begin to take a more holistic view of risk in order to efficiently manage the risks they assume, the capital they deploy, and the checks and balances necessary to regulate those strategies. Any given strategy, for example, consumes a certain amount of capital. A commercial bank focused on the transactions business requires far less capital then an investment firm concentrating on principal trading. Why? Because each strategy has *different risks*. Clearly, there is significantly less risk involved in performing delivery versus payment transactions than in taking investment positions for your own account. Therefore, only by taking a more holistic view, thinking simultaneously of risk, capital, and strategy, can one put appropriate checks and balances into place.

A Story of Risk: Part 6

Max's life as an accountant was mostly a matter of collecting, comparing, and presenting numbers according to Generally Accepted Accounting Principles (GAAP). His work was governed by specific technical requirements, which varied from industry to industry, as well as larger principles—consistency, relevance, reliability, and comparability—which applied to all industries. Consistency meant following a certain set of rules, reporting period by reporting period, so that the bottom line at the end of each quarter, for instance, was reached using the same methods. Relevance meant that the numbers he collected had to be meaningful—that is, the hard numbers of sales, inventory, and costs, not the soft numbers of projections— so that they could be used to evaluate the true financial health of the company. Reliability meant that if another accountant were to repeat the work—in the same way a breakthrough in science must be independently repeatable before it is accepted—the results would be (nearly) identical. Finally, comparability meant that by following the particular accounting standards for each industry, another person could easily evaluate two companies within that industry using the same terms.

The interim audits Max did during the year weren't as painstaking, of course. During those audits, it was enough to know that controls were in place, basic processes were being followed, and therefore that viable numbers were being produced. At the end of the year, though, the numbers had to tally, and if they didn't Max needed to know why.

Just the week before he had come across an obvious case of fraud, involving the owner of a supermarket who had decided that for the past year he would report the proceeds of only four of the checkout aisles in his store, reserving what came in at the fifth for himself. After Max made his report, alerting the owner that he couldn't certify the results, he heard that the investigators sent to the supermarket found only the four checkout aisles the owner had reported. When they looked a little more closely, however, they were able to see the "footprint" of another aisle still visible on the worn linoleum. After a short discussion, aided by the testimony of a cashier who'd been let go for showing up late to work, the owner was convinced that reporting income in keeping with the previous years' levels was a bargain compared to going to jail.

That case was an easy one to spot, once he'd looked over the earlier returns, but, despite the rules he followed as he did his work, there were still gray areas in every audit, and one afternoon Max found himself staring into just that kind of financial fog.

It seemed odd to Max that he had been given this particular job, because he had little experience in that specific industry. Specialization, in fact, was critical once one reached a certain level in accounting, because each industry had its own quirks, strategies, and historical precedents. Still, his boss had told Max he wanted him to handle it personally, so there was nothing for Max to do but buckle down and do his best. As his boss reminded him, the company was an old and valued client.

Within a day or two of starting the job, however, Max sensed— even before he discovered actual evidence—that something didn't add up. He finally narrowed it down to the company's *contingent liabilities*—that is, anticipated costs for certain events that might or might not occur. They were far lower than they should have been, both as a percentage of the company's gross revenues, and in relation to industry standards. What's more, the numbers were far lower than they had been during the previous year, even though the company was now defending itself against a lawsuit brought by one of its competitors. In short, if they came out on the losing end, they would be liable for substantial losses, but their books pointedly ignored the possibility. What Max did not know—unlike his boss—was that the company, long privately held, was only weeks away from an Initial Public Offering.

Max made his report a few days later. His boss sat there, nodding now and then, and then thanked him and sent him on his way. Just before the end of the day, he walked back into Max's office and returned the report. On top of it was a single sheet of paper with what his boss called "recommendations." By the time Max read halfway down the sheet he realized that he was being asked to certify the contingent liabilities *exactly as the company had stated them*. He got up to look for his boss, but by that time he was nowhere to be found.

Max went home that night, talked the incident over with his wife, and the following morning waited outside his boss's office until he was free. With all due respect, Max told his boss, he had performed the audit according to accepted practices, and if Max was going to sign his name to it he couldn't, in good faith, make the requested changes. His boss said he was sorry to hear that, and made it clear that if Max wasn't willing to follow the recommendations, his future at the company was in doubt. Max said that there was no longer any doubt in *his* mind about his future with the company, and promptly gave his boss two weeks' notice.

Risk Principle | 7

HARD WORK

"If you're going through hell, keep going."
—Winston Churchill

At the end of a long day you turn into your driveway, and there ahead of you sits your house, light shining through its windows. You perceive your house as a structure—as a unified whole—but it is instead a thing of many pieces, assembled over thousands of hours, until it took shape; until it became a house.

First the land was cleared and graded, and then a foundation was poured. Next, the frame was thrown up, and the roof was shingled. Once the frame was sheathed with plywood, the windows and doors were hung, the plumbing and electrical work was done, and the interior walls were insulated and covered with sheetrock. As one group of craftsmen covered the seams with tape and spackle, another worked outside, nailing clapboard to the sheathing. A third group lay wooden flooring, and when they had finished, another group sanded the floors and applied coats of polyurethane. Carpenters then nailed trim molding around the doors and windows, and they were followed by painters. Cabinets, fixtures, and appliances were then installed, while landscapers planted trees and seeded the lawn. By that time, a real estate agent had already listed the property for sale.

By the time you drove down the road, weeks later, and looked up the driveway for the first time, all you could see was a finished house. If, however, you were able to look through the eyes of the tradespeople who built it, you would see not a house, but the countless hours of hard work that went into building it.

Managing risk never ends. Eventually, you just run out of time. While you're at it, though, managing risk requires hard work. This is true whether you manage the risk yourself, or pay someone else to do it for you. It is true whether or not you want—or can—perform the research necessary to continually fine tune your portfolio yourself, or whether you give the job to someone else. Most investors choose the latter course, but few of them understand that their jobs do not end once they've put their assets in someone else's hands.

Most of us, in fact, mistakenly believe that a plan, once put into place, no longer requires our attention. But a plan is just words on a piece of paper, and without someone to put it into action, and to rewrite it when necessary, it's something like a car without a driver, speeding straight ahead, down a curving road.

The truth is that many of us don't have the work ethic on which successful planning depends. Others of us quit at the first sign of trouble and never achieve our goals. Success is the child of perseverance—you need to *work* at realizing your goals, and work at them steadily, almost as involuntarily as you breathe, and almost as frequently as you eat and drink. Those of us who succeed never file our plans away—we keep them out on our desks, glance at them whenever we have a free moment, and pencil in possible changes almost every day.

Examples of the success of this approach are all around us. Ask a good money manager what she thinks of German bonds and you won't have to wait for an answer. Continually reexamining asset classes, both domestic and foreign, is her job; she'll have an answer for you because she's always asking *herself* the same question. Spend an evening in a jazz club, but as you listen spellbound to a tenor saxophonist improvising without any apparent thought, don't be fooled into thinking that the solo just popped into his head. Like all great solos, it is the result of relentless practice; and the solo isn't just snatched out of the melody that particular evening, it's a recombination of bits and parts of other solos he's played over the years. Ask a skilled martial artist what he's thinking as he avoids an attack, and then counterattacks, and he'll tell you "nothing." He works constantly at his art, develops muscle memory, and then, when he needs to defend himself, moves *without* thinking. His evasion and counterstrike may appear to be as effortless as the saxophonist's solo, but it too is the result of continual work.

The same sort of work ethic should extend to the continual reexamination of our goals. In the same way a skilled investment manager continually rebalances a client's portfolio, adjusting it in response to the uneven returns of its various parts and shifting market conditions, we must continually reassess our goals as our circumstances change. Has an ageing parent put additional demands on your income, your assets, or your time? Has a summer vacation led to thoughts of owning a house in a warmer climate? Is a daughter about to be married, or have you decided to set up a trust for your grandchildren? The point is that as your responsibilities and goals change, you must continually reassess the risk necessary to satisfy and achieve them. Sound decision making doesn't depend on epiphanies—that is, from sudden, unanticipated insights—it comes from the continual reappraisal of your goals and requirements, followed by corresponding changes in allocations, and the reevaluation of risk. In other words, de-risking your future requires unrelenting work.

Today, many investors attempt to avoid some of this work by adopting a "passive" investing strategy, or one in which their assets automatically track a specific equity or fixed-income index. This approach, though, may require almost the same amount of *monitoring* that active investments do. A savvy investor's total portfolio, for instance, will still be unequally divided between stock index funds and bond index funds—depending on investment goals, time frame, and risk appetite—in order to avoid concentration risk. And all stock and bond funds are not created alike.

The Vanguard 500 index fund, for instance, allocates its assets across the 500 companies that make up the Standard & Poor's 500. A key factor in this investing strategy is the extremely low cost of investing, the result of far lower management costs because research is unnecessary, and trading is infrequent. Where a hedge fund typically charges investors 2 percent and 20 percent—that is, an annual charge of 2 percent of assets under management (AUM), as well as 20 percent of returns, sometimes after a predetermined "hurdle" has been superceded—and a typical money manager charges anywhere from 2 to 2½ percent of AUM, the Vanguard 500's expense ratio, in the winter of 2010, was lower than 0.2 percent, or *one-tenth* of the amount charged by the money manager.*

---

* Mutual fund expense ratios do not ordinarily include the additional costs of trading and transaction fees, although an index fund, by its nature, is a "passive" not an "active" investment.

While the cost benefits of such an approach are obvious, dangers exist in index investing just as they do in any investment strategy, and therefore steady monitoring is required. First, if both domestic and foreign equities markets suffer prolonged losses, index funds will mirror those losses. Second, the indices on which equity index funds are based vary greatly. Some track an extremely large list of broadly varied companies across all sectors, like the Vanguard 500, but with holdings *weighted* in proportion to the index itself. Such a fund might, for instance, be more heavily invested in technology, financial, or energy stocks, and thus be especially sensitive to market conditions in those sectors. Other indices focus on a more narrow group of companies, like the Dow Jones Industrial Average (DJIA), which contains only 30 long-established, U.S., large cap stocks, weighted according to price. As a result, this index will produce results far different than that of, say, the NASDAQ 100, which tracks three times as many companies spread across the industrial, technology, telecommunication, transportation, and insurance sectors—to name but a few. At present, the NASDAQ 100 also includes 15 companies incorporated outside the United States, meaning that it will not necessarily march in lockstep with U.S. markets, as the DJIA does. Concentration risk, then, must be considered when investing passively, although that risk can be addressed by investing in a number of funds.

Finally, the NASDAQ 100 rebalances its index—according to a company's share price and outstanding shares—only once a year. (A company's place can be lost at any time during the year, though, if its index weighting—that is, its value relative to the entire index— falls below .01 percent.) In some cases, then, as a company's share price rises rapidly, it can assume a larger position in the index—and if that company's share price falls rapidly, will be responsible for outsized losses to the index as a whole.

In other words, these indices are not chiseled in stone. While changes in the DJIA are infrequent, one need only consider the delisting of General Motors to understand that no company can consider its place safe over the long term. So, while passive investing unquestionably lowers costs, it too, like any investment strategy, requires constant monitoring, as well as contingency plans for shifts in the market, to say nothing of changes in an investor's goals or risk appetite.

Active investment managers are well aware of the *cost benefit* of passive investing, and thus seek to exceed not only the return on certain indexes—which, in essence, serve as their benchmarks—but also the additional costs associated with proprietary research and active trading. To succeed, they must take risks passive investors do not, either by choosing specific stocks or by favoring certain sectors over others. As a result this approach requires far more attention to portfolio risk, both in terms of the potential for loss, and the likelihood of market-beating gains. Too little risk, therefore, may lead to insufficient returns—relative to the performance of the benchmark, *plus* the costs of active investing—while too much risk may lead to losses that endanger a client's long-term goals, as well as the reputation of the investment manager.

Both of these approaches, of course, must take the investor's requirements into account—that is, whether the investor needs to draw from his investments in order to maintain his lifestyle, or whether he can allow his assets to grow untouched. Younger investors tend to seek long-term gains in tax-deferred accounts, taking advantage of the benefits of compounding for their retirement needs, which are still far in the future, or for their children's college accounts, which will be used over the shorter term. Older investors, instead, no longer in the workforce, may attempt to live off the *proceeds* of their investments, or may plan to draw against them over time. For those investors, tax considerations and the effect of inflation—on top of any changes in the markets—may require them to change their lifestyles year by year, or risk exhausting their savings. Conversely, defined pension benefits, annuity payments, or inheritances may allow older investors to adopt longer-term strategies despite their age. Finally, if an older investor hopes to leave his heirs a legacy, he must constantly compare the cost of his lifestyle with his investment returns with that goal in mind. The point, once again, is that whether you manage your investments yourself, or have others do it for you, paying close attention to the performance of your holdings, given your goals and requirements, is work that never ends.

Even if your personal financial future is secure—to the extent that your assets far exceed your projected needs over the remaining years of your life—conservatively investing your holdings may interfere with other goals, like charitable giving. If that is the case, then a whole new calculus is necessary to achieve your goals—even if you can afford to maintain your lifestyle in spite of short-term market fluctuations, taxes, and inflation. The desire to care for your beneficiaries—say, your children or your grandchildren—requires yet another round of decisions. And these last two goals—that is, charitable giving and legacies—may be served by a single strategy, that of creating a charitable trust. Such an approach can satisfy your charitable goals, and by moving funds out of your hands, greatly reduce the estate taxes your beneficiaries will have to pay. The point, once again, is that no matter the nature of your assets, the cost of your lifestyle, and your other financial goals, continual reevaluation—that is, hard work—is necessary to de-risk your plans.

In the corporate sphere, decision making requires the same amount of hard work, and is complicated by the same factors that concern individual investors—that is, time frame and risk appetite. That said, while individual investors must consider only their own goals, pension plans, for instance, must by law consider the effects of their decisions on those who depend on these benefits. These goals are most efficiently met when well-understood, fixed processes govern the work, as opposed to a dependence on culture. Process puts bodies on the line of scrimmage; culture steps back in the pocket and throws a long pass. And while culture has scored many a touchdown, as the clock ticks down in the fourth quarter process is more likely to win the game. Furthermore, when events jar the markets, and there is little time to think, companies, just like martial artists, do better to rely on process, not culture. Process involves procedures, checkpoints, and proper checks and balances; it does not rely on culture, or personality. What's more, if company culture led to a series of high-risk, low-return positions, how could that same culture be trusted to find a solution to the problem for which *it* was responsible? Throughout my career, whenever I saw a corporation ignoring process, and relying instead on its culture, a red flag slowly unfurled in my mind. And at Citibank in the late 1980s, the gathering storm winds in the commercial real estate market caused that flag to fly like a kite.

By 1989, the Reagan economy had begun to slow down, the savings and loan crisis had led to numerous bank failures, and commercial real estate values had declined precipitously. While the downturn afflicted virtually every bank in the country, Citibank was in an especially difficult position because the problems brewing in its commercial real estate portfolio weren't fully understood until it was too late to do anything about them—that is, other than tally the losses. As then CEO John Reed put it midway through the year, the bank was "getting unduly transaction-oriented." In other words, the bank had focused on generating fees, not on evaluating the long-term consequences of credit decisions, and as real estate values fell, the bank's losses mounted. And when federal regulators, equally late to the game, finally began to police the entire banking sector, they too closed the vaults long after the money was gone, and in the process all but closed the market for commercial real estate too.

Citibank's problems weren't limited to real estate. It also began to suffer devastating losses on a series of poorly conceived Leveraged Buyouts (LBO). As a result, its earnings, share price, and debt rating plunged, and the cost of borrowing skyrocketed. And as other major banks made ever larger provisions for loan losses, Citibank was forced to follow suit, further depleting its capital. Over the next year, it seemed that every quarterly statement included new trouble in yet another of Citibank's divisions. The credit card business wasn't spared, nor were residential real estate loans or the bank's loans to Less Developed Countries (LDC). As a result, by the end of 1991 Reed had no choice but to discontinue dividends for the first time in almost 180 years.

Just as federal regulators had missed signs of trouble across the entire sector, no one at Citibank had looked at the big picture until it was too late. Loan officers had monitored individual transactions, most of which had dotted "i's" and crossed "t's," but somehow no one farther up the corporate ladder noticed that the bank itself had accumulated $13 billion in commercial real estate just as the market was about to go into a free fall. Due diligence was performed deal by deal, but there was no process in place to measure total liability.

As a result, in the early 1990s, when Citibank was still reeling from its huge portfolio of nonperforming commercial real estate loans, CEO John Reed walked into my office and handed me a single piece of graph paper. There were six boxes on it, labeled Corporate Credit, Consumer Credit, Counterparty Risk, Market Risk, Liquidity Risk, and Trading Risk. "Get me a consolidated report," he told me, "and get it to me in three days. I'm pulling my sword out of its sheath, drawing a line in the sand, and letting the board know how I'm going to manage this company going forward."

Under the pressure of that deadline I did nothing but work and eat—sleeping only when I could no longer work—and three days later I delivered the report Reed had requested. He then made his presentation to Citibank's Board of Directors. The Executive suites were on the second floor of 399 Park Avenue, occupying an entire New York City block. I will never forget the way Reed yelled at me across that football field–sized floor after he had made his presentation. "Hey Martin, you done good!"

I had looked at the boxes he had sketched out on that single sheet of graph paper and had seen windows instead, and the Enterprise Risk Management (ERM) system I developed—the company's, and perhaps the industry's first—became known as Windows on

Risk. I continually refined the process over the next six years, and am proud to say that on my watch, even though Citibank steered through exceptionally treacherous waters, it never hit any serious icebergs. During the 1990s, we called the Asian and Russian Financial Crises well before they hit, and we worked our way out of a lot of smaller problems before they assumed dangerous proportions.*

After leaving Citibank, I maintained a friendship with Bill Rhodes, a Vice-Chair of Citibank during my years there and a man for whom I have the deepest respect. In the early years of the twenty-first century he shared an office suite with Sandy Weil, then CEO of Citigroup, and Bob Rubin, former Secretary of the Treasury under Clinton and Chairman of Citibank's Executive Committee. One day, after Bill and I had discussed Citigroup's circumstances over a long lunch, he took me into the C-suite, where members of senior management told me how thankful they were that the bank had Windows on Risk. While I appreciated the praise, what they didn't know was that Bill had told me that same day that the bank, over his objections, had all but stopped using it.

The following day I sold all my shares in Citigroup. As far as I was concerned, the bank's risk management function was doomed to failure. That decision wasn't personal, it was all about process— or, I should say, the lack of process. I saw a style based solely on personal judgment, and believed then as I do today that without a disciplined, rigorous, process-based approach to risk management,

---

* Ten years later, as Chief Risk Officer for one of the world's largest investment firms, my approach had evolved considerably. While I hadn't given up on ERM, I had come to believe that while risk management had to have a seat in the boardroom, it also had to be practiced by everyone in the organization.

disaster would eventually strike. The bank's subsequent performance never gave me cause to regret selling my shares.

Nonetheless, my experiences at Citibank were an invaluable part of my risk management education, and some of them are still bearing fruit today. I often think, when reviewing my career, of a project I was assigned while working at Citibank in the mid-1980s. In short, I was asked to assess the overall Japanese threat to U.S. business, and in particular, the threat Japanese financial institutions posed to Citibank. I spent weeks in Japan studying the economy, the banking system, and the culture. I attended a Shinto ceremony, and several Kabuki performances, a form of theater that many believe is crucial to understanding the psyche of the Japanese people.

I came back to the United States deeply worried. Everything I had seen in Japan convinced me that their business culture presented a serious, long-term competitive threat. In other words, I thought the Japanese were going to cream us, and when delivering my report I didn't sugarcoat it. Walter Wriston, of whom I have spoken earlier, didn't dispute my findings. Instead, he acknowledged the threat, but suggested I undertake a similar survey of American business culture. As a first step, he sent me to see Carver Mead, a legendary professor at Caltech, and one of the fathers of microelectronics.

I had dinner with Mead in the gorgeous, wood-paneled faculty dining room at Caltech. Afterward, we walked back to Mead's lab. By then it was almost 11:00 p.m., but I was amazed to see the number of graduate students still at work. I was equally stunned by the nature of their work—bionic eyes and ears. That visit to Mead's lab, as Wriston had guessed it would, gave me hope for the future of the U.S. economy. While the Japanese posed a serious economic threat, due to their team mentality and work ethic, Mead's lab showed me that the United States had a culture of innovation based on a completely different, individual process. Yes, a *group* of students were at work in the lab, but the progress they made was the result of coordinated, *individual* advances—driven, in this case, by graduate students working through the night, each making his or her own contribution. In other words, innovation, too, grows out of process and perseverance.

The value of a steady, workmanlike approach is not confined to strategic considerations, or to day-to-day operations—it also extends to business continuity planning. Such plans are drawn to ensure that work will proceed in the event of any one of a number of disasters, and farsighted companies, therefore, draw up a series of detailed scripts for a variety of emergencies. Simulations involving power blackouts and backup plans, for instance, are constantly performed. Procedures for personnel roll calls and operations checklists are continually tested and reexamined. And during the process of such simulations, some plans are found wanting. Disaster recovery sites, for instance, once considered a critical part of emergency planning, are no longer in vogue. Why? Because experience has taught us that people won't leave their loved ones or their homes in a crisis. Therefore, a new set of tactics are necessary.

Over the years, that sort of evolutionary approach has occurred in health crisis planning. At first, companies sought to circumvent the problem by making their key employees completely functional at home—or, in other words, to be able to move the work to the employees, instead of the employees having to move to the work.

But that approach too had its weaknesses. What if the bulk of the workforce contracted the Asian Flu—and contracted it while in the office? Moving the work to their homes, then, would be pointless. As a result, forward-looking companies have taken yet another step; if the entire workforce in one location, say, is knocked out by the Asian Flu, they are now ready to move their operations to any one of a number of backup locations, one of which, at least, should be staffed by a healthy workforce.

And just as some approaches have been discarded, others have been added. Continuity planning, for instance, is now routinely extended to key suppliers, because if they go out, you go out too.

We do our best work, in short, not when we scramble, but when hard work has *prepared* us to push extraneous factors aside, and to bring all our talents and strengths to bear on a single task. Individuals who perform well in crises—like Captain Chesley Sullenberger, pilot of the ill-fated US Airways flight 1549, which he was forced to ditch in the Hudson River—are not only able to narrow their vision, but to do it on the spot. They can almost instantaneously bring all their abilities to bear on an unanticipated, potentially lethal problem. In such circumstances they do not rely on logic, nor do they really think. Instead, they rely on intuition, and on learned processes and muscle memory, often without even understanding what they are doing.

Performance in a crisis, then, just like the saxophonist's solo, succeeds because of preparation. Law enforcement agents will tell you the same thing. Well-designed drills, performed over and over again, allow peace officers to react without thinking when faced with a crisis. Hard work pays off. And that work never ends.

A Story of Risk: Part 7

The next six months were the most difficult of Max's life. What's worse, they forced him to confront the many mistakes he'd made. He had been making good money, but had assumed that he always would, and as a result he had saved very little. Whatever was left over after the bills were paid had gone into his investments, most of them tax-deferred, and while those investments had done well, he couldn't get to that money without incurring substantial penalties, to say nothing of jeopardizing his long-term plans.

He had networked extensively while at the accounting firm, but his most important contacts worked alongside him, or farther up the corporate ladder. Applying to other accounting firms, he quickly discovered that his former boss had a different story to tell than he did about the events that caused him to quit, and what's more, was eager to discourage anyone who called to check Max's references. Within a few weeks, Max had no choice but to take whatever work he could get, and although he could scarcely believe it, given his college degree, his CPA, and his work experience, he soon found himself managing a restaurant in Brooklyn, not far from where he lived. By the end of his first two weeks at the restaurant he told his wife they'd have to pull their oldest son out of pre-school. Only by working as much overtime as the owner would give him was he able to make enough money to pay the rent and the health insurance.

He went to work each day cursing his luck, even though he knew he'd done the right thing by refusing to play along with his boss at the accounting firm. He couldn't help but beat himself up, though, for not having thought about what he'd do if he needed to change jobs. He'd been so caught up with work that he hadn't set time aside to regularly reappraise his economic position, nor had he made contingency plans for the future. And knowing that he'd endangered his family didn't make it any easier to get through the days.

He hit bottom the day of the monthly poker game. He'd told his wife he wasn't going to go, but she had watched the fatigue and disappointment slowly draw down the corners of his mouth, and so that morning when he left for work she insisted that he go. He needed a break, she said, and who knows, maybe he'd win some money. He hadn't been at the restaurant for an hour when the front door opened and the health inspector came in. There had been a few complaints about rats in the back of the restaurant, and if the alley wasn't spotless by the next morning, the restaurant would be fined. He sent one of the employees out back, but an hour later, when he checked the work, he realized that he had no choice but to do it himself.

Once again, he got to Rob's apartment late, and by the way everyone started to sniff the air when he sat down, he knew the smell of the dirty job he'd had to do wasn't just in *his* nostrils. But that wasn't the worst of it. Rob had been out of work too, but he had just gotten back from Vail, where he'd been skiing with some old friends of theirs from school. When he got back, his father had put him in touch with a stock broker he used to do business with, and said he certainly ought to be willing to give Rob a job, given all the money his father had lost following his stock picks over the years. Rob had an appointment to meet with him the following week, but according to his father, it was a done deal.

The final blow came late in the game. Max was dealt three kings, but one of the other players drew to an inside straight. As Max counted what was left of his chips he realized that he'd lost more or less the same amount of money he'd earned cleaning the garbage cans in the alley that afternoon, and so he told them all he'd had enough, cashed in his chips, and for the rest of his life never gambled again.

PART | 3

DECISION MAKING

Risk Principle | 8

CONSIDER ALL THE
ALTERNATIVES

"Not everything that can be counted counts;
and not everything that counts can be counted."
—Albert Einstein

Change is ongoing. It occurs all around us, ceaselessly. It is so constant, in fact, that we are usually unaware of it, or like the way one season slowly gives way to another, are aware of the change only after it has taken place. Other changes occur so rapidly—that is, in the space of a single day—that we are almost unable to process them. Those who brought us into the world pass out of it. Our children bring their children into the world. And whether those singular, eventful days are cause for sorrow or celebration, our lives are never the same again.

With so much change occurring around us, then, it is one of life's great ironies that we can bring about so little of it ourselves. The sun rises and falls, indifferent to our activities. The weather makes our days, but we cannot make it. Mountains sit placidly in the distance. We cannot move them. The night sky is full of stars, but they are beyond our reach.

And yet every morning, wonderfully ignorant of our insignificance, we rise believing that we can make a difference. And to some extent it is true, for there are decisions to be made, most of them almost meaningless, but some of which may actually change our lives. And it is those decisions to which we turn now.

The changes we *can* make—that is, the decisions that will actually have an impact on our lives—are contained in a vast, confusing universe of alternatives. Fortunately, the least consequential decisions seem to offer the most bewildering array of choices. What should you eat for breakfast? What tie goes with this shirt? Do these shoes work with this dress? As decisions become more important—even incrementally so—they tend to present fewer alternatives.

If you have three or four tasks to complete by day's end, for instance, you'll likely begin by ranking them according to importance, and will begin with the most critical one—or the one you think will require the most time. Even here, though, a poor initial decision won't prevent you from getting the job done—if you make the wrong choice, you'll simply have to work longer to compensate for the mistake.

As more important, longer-term decisions come into the picture, the alternatives shrink even further—but the impact of those decisions will be more powerful, and longer lasting. At this point a more careful review of the alternatives becomes critical. Do you live where you want to live, or just where you happen to find yourself? What will a move cost you, and what opportunities will it offer? Given your talents and your goals, have you chosen the right industry, or even the right profession? Have you put your financial resources to work in such a way that you are likely to reach your goals? Have you weighed the risk of losses against the rewards of gains? Do you have the expertise, the stamina, and the work ethic to manage those resources yourself, or would you be better off putting them in someone else's hands? And if you have chosen the latter course, how frequently should you monitor the results?

As your decisions become more important, it also becomes necessary to take exit strategies into account. A 30-year-old with young children may reasonably risk a job change—if it doesn't work out, she can always look for another. A 50-year-old with children in college and a parent in need of financial assistance, on the other hand, may not have the time to recover from the consequences of a poor career decision. Even a person in their 60s with a well-funded, well-balanced retirement plan should have an exit strategy in the event that certain predetermined inflection points occur in the markets.

A careful review of the available alternatives also leads to the elimination of the most common and unforgivable error in decision making—that of an error of omission. This error occurs when decisions are made *before* all the viable alternatives have been considered—or worse, when *none* of them have been considered. And while a shortened time frame can also cause this sort of error—say, when injuries caused by an accident require immediate surgery, and there is no time to conduct a search for the most qualified specialist in the area—errors of omission are often made offhandedly, despite the existence of real alternatives. Errors of commission, on the other hand—decisions that are made after considering all the alternatives, but nonetheless do not work out—can't be avoided.

Let's consider these principles in light of a serious disease.

Once confronted with irrefutable evidence of your illness you will probably begin to think back over the past few months, and in retrospect will recognize certain events, dismissed at the time, as clear signs of what was to come. But there is no time for remorse. Decisions have to be made, and quickly, because while your condition is serious, the doctor has not given you an immediate death sentence. Yours, let's say, is an aggressive cancer, and has already begun to move inside your body, but treatments exist. Your doctor has a suggestion, of course, but the decision is yours. The most important approach at this stage in your treatment, therefore, is an open discussion of the alternatives and their risks.

If you are able to gather your wits, you will investigate all possible treatments, will consider the reputations of all available physicians and facilities, and barring the existence of a waiting list, you will make a decision and undergo treatment as quickly as possible. If that initial treatment is not effective, you may have time to try another. Whether or not that's necessary, or even possible, you will have done all you could have done once you received news of your illness. If any errors are involved, they are errors of commission. You conducted your research and made a reasoned decision. Whatever the outcome, this approach is vastly better than simply nodding your head when your doctor refers you to a specialist, going home, and not doing anything at all. That is an error of omission, and it is unforgivable—and in the case of cancer, often unforgiving.

Even if you have the time to do your due diligence, first investigating the nature of your cancer, and then searching for those most capable of treating it, it's easy to get lost in the numbers. Do you want the surgeon who has performed the operation you need more often than anyone else in the area, or should you expand your search to neighboring states as well? Or for that matter, across the country, or even around the world? (Keep in mind that the first heart transplant was performed in South Africa.) Should you look for a surgeon with a degree from a prestigious medical school, or a surgeon respected by experts in the field?

Most men and women attempt to bring a sort of mathematical *precision* to their decision making, believing not only that equations for risk assessment exist, but that they can be used to calculate risk just as reliably as the value of x can be determined when the value of y is known. Nearly all of us tend to believe that decisions based on the numbers—rather than instinct, the experiences of our friends, or case histories—lead to far more precise and dependable results. The numbers don't lie, we tell ourselves, and so if we can just suppress our emotions, and remain emotionally aloof during our analysis of the data, our decisions will necessarily be more sound. Therefore we look to numbers—checking statistics, reading back over historical trends, collecting figures and calling them *facts*—believing that if we can *quantify* the factors involved in any given decision, we can more successfully diminish our risk.

If only it were true.

Crucial to this belief is our conviction that the numbers we gather are in fact, *facts*, when nothing could be further from the truth. Sometimes, for example, an entirely random number will skew our research. Recently, for instance, a behavioral psychologist asked people to estimate the percentage of African countries in the UN. Before they answered, however, he spun a roulette wheel in front of them. Respondents who saw a higher number on the roulette wheel also estimated a higher percentage of African countries in the UN, although of course the number on the roulette wheel had nothing to do with the correct answer. Our calculations, in other words, can be easily affected by utterly random numbers. Psychologists call this an *anchoring effect*, or *anchor bias*. And as you de-risk your plans you must keep these biases in mind.

Research in neuroscience, as well as advances in what is called Emotional Intelligence, tell us even more about how our perceptions of numbers and statistics are warped both by our emotions and our internal neurocircuitry. Whether or not the psyche is involved we still tend to have difficulties moving principles of mathematics out of textbooks and applying them to real-world situations. Consider the following, apparently simple problem.

A bridge is one mile long. If a car goes over the first half of the bridge at 30 mph, how fast does it have to go over the second half to average 60 mph? Most people quickly answer 90 mph, but they're wrong. They make this mistake because they don't understand the implications of the first, vital piece of information—that is, that the bridge is only one mile long. So, to average 60 mph, the car *must* complete the trip in one minute. It may go faster or slower during that minute, but in order to achieve an average speed of 60 mph over the one-mile-long bridge, the crossing *must* last exactly one minute. According to the scenario above, though, the driver has already used that minute going over the first half of the bridge, at 30 mph. The correct answer, then, is that the car would have to cross the second half of the bridge *instantaneously*, because time has already elapsed. Therefore it can't go fast enough over the second half of the bridge to average 60 mph.

This is a simple error of understanding, and the truth is that the scenario is a trick of sorts, *designed* to fool you. What makes you think that you'll do better out in the real world, though, if you have very little time to react, or are under intense emotional pressure? Unless you are a trained mathematician, the chances are very small that you'll be able to use complex calculations to aid your decision making.

Finally, it is also true that too great an attention to numbers is often a waste of time. Most times it's better to be *approximately right* than to be *precisely wrong*. The rule is a simple one—don't get carried away by, or take undue comfort in, complex calculations; just make sure you're in the right *ballpark*, instead of trying to get things exactly right.

Two examples in my own career come to mind. When I started working at PWC, a partner customarily reviewed my work at the end of every engagement. One of the first times this happened, the partner who had been assigned to me took a quick look at my work—which I knew to be impeccable—asked me a few probing questions, and told me the review was over. When I asked him why he was so easy on me, he said: "I know that anyone who has taken the time to do their work so neatly has done a thorough job." So, while the audit partner did not check every detail—in fact, he didn't have the time to check every detail—he was experienced enough to know that if I had taken so much care with my presentation, I was, at the very least, *approximately* right about the numbers.

The second example had to do with an estimate of an operational loss. My staff had used a complex model, testing 120 scenarios, and had then handed me the results. I took one look at the bottom line and told them their calculations couldn't possibly be right. They went back to the drawing board, no doubt wondering who I thought I was, but much to their surprise, quickly found an error.

Why did I get it right, while five talented people using a sophisticated risk engine got it wrong? The answer is simple: They trusted their method, while I simply thought about the final number using commonsense and experience. While I didn't do the calculations myself, I approached their work having put some upper and lower bounds around the number I expected to see, used some benchmark losses to get a sense of the likely magnitude, and thus was able to understand the approximate level of the loss without relying on a complex model.

Of course this sort of pattern recognition, which George Moore of Citibank called "being able to recognize the same girl with different clothes," is not fail proof either. In fact, cognitive research by Kahneman and Tversky has shown that the natural human tendency to seek patterns often leads them to see patterns where none exist—or when they exist only over the short term. When a baseball player has two or three hitless games, for instance, the average fan (or sportswriter) will tell you he's in a slump. A look at his average over the course of the past month, however, will almost always come closer to his lifetime batting average, because during that time he will have had two or three other games where he has hit higher than his average. In the same way an American League batter who faces a National League pitcher in the World Series may have a higher or lower batting average against that particular pitcher, but that average will have little meaning because of the small number of times the two have faced each other.

Framing bias, another natural tendency that leads us to attach undue significance to meaningless information, depends on the manner in which we pose questions, or the way we present findings. Though the form of the presentation has no real significance, it often has a significant impact on how we see things. Consider the following example.

A king has a dream. In the dream, he sees one large tree, and many small trees sprouting up all around it. Eventually, all of the small trees die, and the big tree is left standing by itself. When the king awakens, unsure of the dream's meaning, he calls in his two most trusted advisors.

The first interpreted the dream as follows: "Your Majesty, your children are all going to die at an early age, and so no one will succeed you." Upon hearing this, the king promptly had the advisor taken away, and instructed his guards to put the man to death. The second advisor, who had served both the present king and his father before him, stepped forward.

"My king," he said, "the meaning of your dream is clear. You will live a long, long life, a life of such great length that you will outlive all your children." Hearing this, the king was appeased. Both of his royal advisors had described exactly the same scenario, but the second had presented it in a manner more acceptable to the king.

The point is that your perception of risk and your appetite for it can be significantly altered by the manner is which the question is framed. One way to avert framing bias is to consider the question from multiple points of view. In fact, it is often best to reframe the question from the opposing point of view. If, for instance, something is true X percent of the time, it must be false 100–X percent of the time.

We also tend to make fewer errors when mathematical problems are presented in human terms—a propensity first revealed by the Wason Selection Test—which may be the result of natural selection. Complex calculations are not, of course, found in the wild;

the ability to solve them is the result of recent scientific advances, not the result of natural selection. Human judgment, on the other hand, has long been of use as our highly social species evolved.

Consider the following classic Wason Selection task. Each of the shapes or colors below is visible on one side of a playing card. The other side of each card also has one of the four symbols or colors on it (i.e., square, circle, yellow, or red).

Comp: Word spacing should be equal (about 2-ems) between terms in the two term lists following below.

SQUARE   CIRCLE   YELLOW   RED

The question is this: what is the minimum number of cards you must turn over, and which cards are they, to prove the following rule: If a card has a circle on one side, it has the color yellow on the other side?*

Now let's reconsider the same question, but this time using human beings in a familiar setting, rather than numbers and colors (again, right out of Wason's own work). Imagine a bar with four stools. The cards below give you information either about the person sitting on the stool, or the drink in front of them.

BEER   SODA   22 YEARS OLD   17 YEARS OLD

---

* The correct answer is CIRCLE and RED. Turning over either the square, which has nothing to do with the problem, or the yellow, which would not disprove the statement *if* there were a circle on the other side, would not definitively answer the question. The circle, on the other hand, must be turned over to validate the statement—that is, that the flip side is yellow. For the opposite reason the red card must be turned over, to ensure that it does not show a circle. If you got this wrong, welcome to the club. Approximately one in four people do.

The question: What is the minimum number of cards you have to turn over, and which cards are they, to prove the following statement: If a person drinks alcohol, they must be at least 21 years old.*

The point, once again, is that we are imperfectly reasoning beings, and that solutions to even relatively simple problems of probability and mathematics are often beyond our abilities. In much the same way we also tend to trust scenarios with more, rather than fewer details, whether or not the additional details actually assist us in understanding the situation. Psychologists refer to this as *representation bias.* Take the following example: Over the next year, Treasury bill yields will rise more than 50 basis points, and global equities will rise more than 10 percent. While there is certainly a chance that these two events will occur simultaneously, it is far easier to judge the probability of each occurring on its own. And yet we are naturally drawn to more complicated scenarios, even if they actually cloud our reasoning. As a result, when de-risking our plans we must continually guard against these natural biases. (Representation bias also figures prominently in the psychology of *lying.* As any parent knows, children are far more likely to construct elaborate scenarios when disguising the truth. Practiced liars, on the other hand, know that the best lie is the simplest lie, because it can be challenged on fewer particulars.)

---

* In this case, which does not differ logically from the one that preceded it, the answer is Beer and 17-years-old. You needn't turn over the soda card, because it does not figure in the statement, nor the 22-years-old card, since whether that person is drinking beer or soda the statement would still remain in question. For reasons unknown, however, respondents are far more likely to solve this problem correctly.

Sunken costs—or sunk costs—are yet another example of the obstacles our psychological makeup presents to sound decision making. A sunken cost is one that has already been incurred, and cannot be recovered. Let's say, for example, that you've bought tickets to the theater. Days later, however, you hear from friends that the show is a waste of time. If you cannot consider the cost of the tickets to be *sunken*—that is, already paid for—then you'll go to the show even though you're unlikely to enjoy it. If, however, you can view the decision rationally, the sunken cost of the tickets is no reason for you to waste an evening—to say nothing of the costs of dinner, parking, and the opportunity cost of your lost time. Badly fitting shoes are another example. Simply because you have paid for a new pair of ill-fitting shoes, does it make sense to wear them until your feet are blistered? Finally, to consider a far more serious example, if a military incursion has already cost the lives of 5,000 soldiers, does it make sense to risk the lives of other soldiers simply to justify the earlier deaths?

Research has also shown that people value what they own about twice as much as others do. This is called the endowment effect. Some of this natural inclination may be attributable to a fear of the unknown. That is, I know how well off I am now, and changing my circumstances—or selling something to which I attach a certain value, even though others consider it less valuable—would leave me psychologically worse off than before. This natural bias has profound implications for risk management and investment strategy, because when investors put a higher value on their possessions or investments than the market does, it often leads them to hold on to them far longer than they should, with disastrous effects. One morning, for instance, looking to rebalance your portfolio, you call your broker and ask how much your stake in American Electro-Widget is worth. The stock, you are told, is trading in the 80s. You, however, bought it for $100 per share and so you can't bear to part with it. In the market of your mind, the stock is still worth *at least* as much as you paid for it—no matter what the market—or the observable price—tell you. Another explanation for this type of behavior is that human beings are naturally more willing to recognize their successes than their failures—and selling shares for less than you bought them would force us to recognize a failure.

The endowment effect obviously has deep psychological underpinnings, and that brings us back to the role of emotion in decision making. Earlier in these pages I spoke about the way wise decision makers check their emotions at the door, and yet study after study shows that when stock traders make financial decisions their blood pressure spikes, their palms become sweaty, and they breathe more quickly. This constitutes one more nail in the coffin of the Efficient Market Hypothesis, which not only presumes that buyers and sellers will make decisions based on readily available, reliable information, but that they will do so rationally and dispassionately. The truth, of course, as most of us know, is that we often make financial decisions—especially over the short term—in a highly emotional state. This is not necessarily a bad thing, because our emotional and rational vectors can actually work in sync. It's bad, in short, only when our emotions *overcome* our reason, instead of working alongside it. When that happens, we need to take a step back.

Taken together, these biases encourage us to hold our investment positions far longer than we should, and to shun reasonable risk even while being willing to risk far larger losses in the pursuit of far greater gains. Our natural inclinations, therefore, lead us to take gains sooner than we should, missing much of the potential for gain in our investments, and to accept continuing losses long after we should have exited our positions, extending the potential for loss on our investments.

I am reminded of a former colleague at Citibank who, like I, received stock options as part of his compensation. He was a loyalist, even after he left the company, and he rode the stock down to $1 per share. Having worked at the company for many years, he was emotionally attached to his options, and put a far higher value on them than the market did. As a result, he was willing to incur losses a more objective man would easily have avoided.

It may be helpful at this point to consider two more approaches to decision making, each the opposite of the other. In the first, a decision is made more or less intuitively, followed by an attempt to assemble facts to support it. In the second, the facts are gathered first, then analyzed, and a decision is finally reached. To begin, it is easy to see that the time frames of the two protocols differ greatly. The first can be accomplished much more quickly; the second requires more time. Scientists, for example, cannot afford to use the first approach. Their methodology must be precise, and their results repeatable. Most successful business consultants, however, approach their work using the first protocol. Senior managers, too, frequently have no choice but to make decisions this way. With little information, and less time, they are forced to attempt shortcuts. Those who know what they're doing, however, also consider exit strategies, in the event that their quick decisions prove to be wrong.

Suppose, for instance, that you are responsible for a power grid, and that you have a capacity problem. If you've thought ahead, you'll have a brown-out strategy—that is, you will have already decided who you'll cut power to first, who will come next, and so on. If disaster hits, then, you'll respond almost automatically. But circumstances may require you to have an exit strategy. What if, for instance, the grid goes down while a football game is being played at a local stadium? Then, you'll want to be able to make a flexible response to changing circumstances, and not plunge 50,000 fans into darkness.

Decision making, in other words, is relative, not absolute. Therefore, it is helpful to compare your results to a benchmark. This enables you to remain *committed* to your decisions, regardless of momentary ups and downs, or to realize that it's time to bail out and change your strategy. For this reason, most investment strategies utilize benchmarks, or yard sticks. Alpha—that is, the return in excess of the benchmark—is the most common measurement to determine if an investment advisor has added value. Considered in this light, if a simple market index returns 5 percent, and an actively managed portfolio returns 6 percent, was active management worth it? Most likely, it was not. If you had simply purchased an instrument that replicated the market, you would have earned almost the same return, without having to pay a manager his fees and without having incurred additional transaction costs. In other words, the manager did not provide *alpha* relative to the benchmark.

In investments, then, everything is relative. First and foremost, the performance or return must be judged in relation to the risk involved. In other words, the number you're looking for is not the return, but the *risk-adjusted* return. If, for instance, someone achieves an annual return of 5 percent using complex derivative strategies, rather than making 5 percent by purchasing U.S. Treasuries, are the returns comparable? They are not, because the level of risk incurred in the derivatives strategy is far greater than the nearly risk-free return earned from Treasuries. For greater risk, one expects a greater return. But do not be mistaken—there is no return without risk. Again, as Walter Wriston said: "Risk may be a four letter word, but there's nothing wrong with it—as long as it's properly managed."

Finally, when making decisions we need to consider the difference between poor outcomes—after all available information was gathered, and considered in light of our goals—and bad decisions. It may help to consider a typical round of golf.

In my experience, hitting ten strokes over your handicap is usually the result of four or five bad shots—and five or six bad *decisions*. These poor decisions generally occur because we do not honestly consider our abilities. Let's say your tee shot landed right in the middle of the fairway, 190 yards from the flag, but your second shot took a bad hop and left you to one side of the green. If, to further complicate matters, a deep bunker with a steep wall lies between you and the elevated green, getting on safely means lifting the ball ten feet in the air, and then stopping it right next to the flag. At that point, you've got to ask yourself if that's a shot you can make. Sure, you'll add at least one shot to your round by chipping out in front of the green, and then taking another shot at the hole, but attempting the shot from where you lie after two, and failing, might leave you in the trap, or on the other side of the green in even worse shape. In other words, before taking the shot, you have to ask yourself if it's worth the risk, given your abilities.

A Story of Risk: Part 8

Max's wife, Barbara, had a history of colon cancer in her family—both her grandfather and her father died from the disease. Her grandfather was simply unlucky; the disease killed him before early detection was made possible by advances in medicine. Her father, however, was more focused on earning a living than worrying about his health, and so ignored his doctor's recommendation that as a high-risk patient he should undergo a colonoscopy. By the time Barbara's father's cancer was discovered, it had already metastasized into his lymph nodes, his liver, and his lungs, and there was nothing to do but make him as comfortable as possible during his final months. He died a month before his 54th birthday, leaving his widow with a $100,000 insurance policy, no steady income, and two mortgages on their house.

Though Barbara had not reached the age at which an initial screening for colon cancer is recommended, her mother, distraught over her husband's untimely death, convinced her daughter to make an appointment with a gastroenterologist. As the day of the examination approached, however, Barbara became more and more afraid that the doctor would discover evidence of the disease that had killed her father, and the thought unnerved her. On the day before the exam, after a sleepless night, she told her husband she wasn't going. Max, not a worrier by nature, tried to talk her into honoring her commitment, but when he saw she wasn't going to change her mind he called the doctor's office and offered to take the appointment himself. He, too, was younger than the age at which the exam is routinely recommended, and what's more, no one in his family had a history of the disease. Why, then, was he so eager to take his wife's place? The answer was simple. He didn't want to pay for the appointment if no one showed up, something he'd have to do since his wife canceled at the last minute. So he drank the liquid that night, took a cab to the doctor's the next morning—his wife wouldn't go anywhere near the place—and before long he was on the table.

The results of the colonoscopy were negative. That morning, however, just before the anesthesiologist put Max under, the gastro-enterologist, having read through Max's medical history and seen that he suffered from acid reflux, recommended another exam as well—an esophagogastroduodenoscopy—or scoping of the mouth, throat, esophagus, stomach, and duodenum. Max, acutely aware of costs given his present circumstances, asked if having the two procedures done that morning would save him any money. The doctor told him it would save him the cost of an additional deduct-ible payment—instead of one for both treatments—to say nothing of time and trouble.

The gastroenterologist found no signs of trouble in Max's mouth, throat, esophagus, or stomach, but as he moved the scope into Max's duodenum he stopped, leaned in closer to the screen, and saw what was clearly an early-stage adenocarcinoma.

Once Max had been brought back to his senses, he got dressed, wobbled into the waiting room, and asked the receptionist to call him a cab. As he sat there, he began to think over his plans for the rest of the day. He wasn't expected at work until 4:00 p.m., and so he figured he'd go home and put a few more resumes in the mail. He was beginning to feel like a shipwrecked sailor, writing mes-sages in bottles and throwing them out beyond the breakers, but he knew he had to keep trying. If he didn't find another job soon, he'd have no choice but to break into his 401(k).

The look on the doctor's face, however, quickly turned his thoughts away from his finances. Once he'd taken a seat in the doctor's office, and had listened to the extent of the bad news, his thoughts turned to his health insurance—and then to his life insurance.

The doctor wasted no time before discussing the next steps. In short, there was no time to lose. The disease was extremely rare, especially in a nonsmoking, nondrinking man in his early 40s, and yet there was little doubt about the diagnosis. The doctor wanted to follow the scope with a biopsy—and the sooner the better—but he didn't gave Max much hope. There was little chance the tumor would turn out to be benign. The only question was the stage—or put another way, whether the cancer had already begun to spread into the surrounding tissue.

By the time Max got out of the cab in front of his house, he was a little steadier on his feet, but he still hadn't figured out how he was going to tell his wife. The funny thing was that the idea of spending the rest of his life managing a restaurant didn't seem so bad anymore.

Once he'd kissed his wife, and had told Barbara that the *colonoscopy* had been negative—which was true—he went to his computer and Googled "adenocarcinoma of the duodenum." Over 300,000 results came up. He sat back in his chair, reached for the phone, called the restaurant and told the day manager he wouldn't be able to come in because of the lingering effects of the anesthesia, but that he'd be in the following day. And then he went to work.

By the time he and his family had finished dinner, and he and his wife had gotten the boys into bed, he was ready to talk. He didn't attempt to minimize the news. It wasn't good, but there were two ways to look at it. If Barbara hadn't decided to cancel her appointment, the tumor almost certainly wouldn't have been discovered until it had progressed much further. And based on the initial, visual inspection, the doctor believed it was still in the early stages. They'd know more once they got the results of the biopsy, but until they did, there was no reason to consider the worst case.

What's more, four hours of Internet research had acquainted Max with the basics of the disease, and its treatment, and if the doctor's initial diagnosis was confirmed, viable surgical options existed. The important things to remember, he told his wife—once she had finally stopped crying—was that he was in good health otherwise, they had good medical insurance, and they lived in a place where experienced specialists and top-flight facilities were plentiful. He just had to decide who to put his trust in. He also had to decide between two alternatives: a surgery focused only on the affected area—the duodenum—or the Whipple procedure, which involved removing portions of his stomach, the first and second portions of the duodenum, the common bile duct, the head of the pancreas— because it shares its blood supply with the duodenum—and the gallbladder. The first, obviously, was a far less complicated procedure, but it left open the possibility that the surrounding organs had been affected, a danger the Whipple procedure reduced.

Rob, who of course had no idea what Max was going through, had decisions of his own to make. A week after he started his new job, Lisa made it clear to him that it was time he started shopping for a wedding ring. He told her that while he agreed—in principle—he thought it would be a much better idea if they waited, you know, until he could put a little money away. She said she couldn't wait any longer, and to make her point showed him the results of a home pregnancy test.

Risk Principle | 9

RISK IS EVERYONE'S RESPONSIBILITY IN THE DECISION-MAKING PROCESS

"The difference between involvement and commitment
is like an eggs-and-ham breakfast: The chicken was involved,
but the pig was committed."

—Anonymous

Imagine a beautiful summer day. You are having a picnic. You leisurely munch on a delicious sandwich, and wash it down with a glass of cold lemonade. The sun beats down, your stomach is full, and before long you are stretched out on your back. You close your eyes for just a moment, basking in the warmth, and without planning to do it, you fall asleep for a good hour. Awakening, well rested, you turn your head away from the glare of the sun, and there, next to you on the blanket, you see a long line of ants carrying the crumbs of your sandwich back to their colony.

Ant colonies are frequently used as metaphors for human activity, and despite our unwillingness to compare our own efforts—the result of the organized, collective work of *individuals*, each with his or her own personality and talents—to the mindless labor of thousands of identical ant *workers*, the metaphor is useful when examining the nature of large social organisms. The Queen ant, in short, does not direct activity from above—the workers are genetically programmed to perform their tasks in accordance with the *mission* of the colony, and on the day of your picnic they simply follow those primal directives, methodically marching the remnants of your sandwich away without any supervision.

At the end of the 1990s, I became the CEO of a hedge fund, a job for which I believed I was eminently qualified, given my understanding of the macroeconomic environment and my lengthy experience running a trading desk and managing risk. In the CEO's seat for the first time in my life, however, I quickly realized that the typical command and control structures used to manage large financial institutions—including the Enterprise Risk Management (ERM) system I had helped create at Citibank—somehow came up short. They did not effectively promote risk management *throughout* the organization. Something else was needed. In other words, I realized that effectively de-risking your plans requires the same sort of enterprise-wide commitment one sees in an ant colony.

This is not to say that ERM should be discarded, only that it needs to be reinforced with a bottom-up—or side-to-side—component as well. In other words, effective risk management can only succeed with a *comprehensive* process in place, beginning with the investor, continuing on to the investment manager, and then fanning out through every level of the enterprise. A top-down approach may have satisfied investors' and regulatory agencies' concerns regarding risk—even when some used it only to create the *illusion* of controls—but once the buck stopped with me I quickly realized that it was incapable of addressing the wide variety of risks that arise in the day-to-day operations of a buy-side financial institution. Neither does such an approach provide a true measurement of the company's aggregate risk—for which the company's senior management is justly responsible—because it does not effectively treat the risks involved with every transaction *as they occur.* For that to happen, risk management cannot be considered a police function performed only by an institution's senior management and risk management staff, it must instead become *embedded* in every level of the organization. Put another way, the principles of risk management cannot be enforced—they must be *applied.* To understand why this is so, it is helpful to look at the history of ERM, and at the nature of buy-side operations.

ERM grew out of the regulatory environment of the early 1990s, partly in response to a pattern of fraudulent financial reporting—for which mostly accounting firms, and not senior management, could then be held legally responsible—and partly because of financial crises brought about by the misuse of new, poorly understood financial instruments like derivatives. Sarbanes-Oxley was the legislative response to the first, and ERM was the industry's response to the second. Citibank's Windows on Risk, discussed earlier in this book, was an early example of an ERM program—in fact, it may have been the first. That approach, however—at least at Citibank—based on in-depth research within discreet risk categories, scenario construction, and action plans related to those scenarios, was eventually abandoned. And the results speak for themselves.

Again, this does not mean that ERM should not have a place at management's table, only that, as its title makes clear, it is designed for *enterprise*-wide control functions, the evaluation of new financial products (and their suitability for specific portfolios), disaster recovery and information security—not for inculcating a culture of risk management that extends all the way down to the transactional level.

Such top-down control functions, in fact, are far better suited to sell-side organizations—that is, banks, investment banks, and brokers—which take proprietary positions that require approvals/ oversight at the transactional level. For that reason, an independent risk management function has long been a part of sell-side management. In the early 1990s, however, that sell-side role began to migrate to the buy side—that is, mutual funds, complexes, and asset management companies. It can be argued, however, that applying sell-side risk controls to buy-side operations not only doesn't promote risk management, under certain conditions it can actually impede it. A quick look at VaR—or value at risk—helps explain why.

VaR is the amount of money a specific investment can lose in a single day. Traditionally used to measure the value at risk on *discrete* transactions, it has now begun to be applied across entire portfolios. Its strength is that it is easily calculated. Its weakness, if it has one, is that it is based on historical loss data, which do not necessarily reflect current conditions. For that reason, it can provide you—and regulators, I might add—with a false sense of security. VaR is also a poor indicator during extreme events—it tells you the best likely outcome, not the worst.

And these limitations, when VaR is applied across entire portfolios, reveal the weaknesses of what is otherwise a valuable transactional tool. Without a doubt, VaR *can* be used to predict the total potential loss in a diversified portfolio over the course of single day. And while that aggregate VaR is interesting, and somewhat useful, the buy side is constrained by the client's mandates—that is, the responsibility of the buy side is to serve clients according to their expressed goals and risk appetites. Therefore, if a fund's objective is long-term performance, say over a specific business cycle, the amount the entire portfolio can lose on a single day is an ineffective way to judge a portfolio's management. Such a measurement might, in fact, encourage a portfolio manager to make poor *long-term* decisions—the basis of all sound investments—because of potential, not actual, short-term losses.

Seen in this light, top-down, or portfolio-wide general measurements do not necessarily optimize decisions at the individual portfolio level. In fact, it is far preferable to encourage the portfolio manager to be a risk manager himself, and to think of the risk involved every time he adjusts a client's portfolio—again, always in light of the client's expressed wishes, investment time frame, and risk appetite. Furthermore, if everyone in the organization considers himself a risk manager, when the portfolio manager makes a trade, the traders will also understand the risk implications of the execution of the trade, as well as the risk involved with the counterparty on the *other* side of the trade. If this is so, the back office personnel will also understand the operational risk implications of the trade, and ensure that it does not fail because of improper trade instructions, or because, say, the foreign exchange component of the trade was not done in a timely manner. It is for this reason that a *culture of risk management*, permeating the entire organization, will not so much *outperform* top-down controls, but will instead *add* to their effectiveness.

As effective as such an approach can be, it cannot be implemented overnight, even with the support of senior management. Although process-driven, it requires a broad cultural change within an organization.

Cultures, in fact, migrate from company to company, and my career is a good example. While I was intimately involved with the creation of what might be called the first stage of ERM, my approach to enterprise-wide risk management has evolved over the years as I have moved from job to job, gaining additional experience along the way. As a risk manager at Citibank, my *signature*, which was withheld until I did my due diligence and was comfortable that the bank was protected, was required for any transaction. My approval, in fact, was *part* of the transaction process, not divorced from it, or brought to bear only after the fact. Only when I moved to the top rung of the management ladder myself, however, did I realize the limitations of such an approach. It wasn't enough for upper-level management to monitor the risk involved in any given decision, because the chain of command was too long, the goals of the various departments were too varied, and the level of activity was too high for active control from the top. Instead, it became clear that unless every portfolio manager and every trader employed the fundamentals of risk management—in every aspect of the investment process—the company as a whole could not effectively manage risk. This was especially true on the buy side, where an advisor could easily follow the investor's guidelines, and yet incur great risk. In other words, if the person making the transaction on behalf of the client didn't effectively manage risk, no one could. Therefore, to the extent ERM still exists, I would rename it "Embedded Risk Management."

This is as true for individual investors as it is for individuals within a larger organization. And while you can't sit across the desk from your investment advisor and approve every change he or she makes in your portfolio, there is no substitute for doing the due diligence to determine that the risk culture of the company you invest with is consistent with *your* risk appetite. This is especially true once you accept the fact that your goals will change as your life changes, and that those revisions will occur as economic conditions change around you.

This is not to say that ordinary investors can match wits with fund managers, whose experience, focus, and access to proprietary research separate them from average stock pickers. While the principles of risk management are based on commonsense, their application across large portfolios can be tortuously difficult, to say nothing of treacherous. What's more, after years of experience, some money managers develop a sixth sense regarding their positions.

During the tech boom, for instance, when the volatility of stock price movement was literally off the historic charts, our hedge fund purchased a tech stock that shot up like a rocket. Rather than ride the surge past its peak, however, the responsible trader sold the stock one day and then came into my office to report. I was stunned, and I told him so. Like most investors holding the stock I thought it still had fuel in its tanks, and that he had sold it while the afterburners were still firing. He didn't agree.

"I've been watching this stock for three weeks," he said, "and I've tracked every single tick of the price, up and down. Last week, though, I started to see signs that it is losing its momentum. Trust me, it's about to fall."

Sure enough, the price of the stock began to decline a day or two after our discussion. Of course that trader isn't as successful every time he exits a position. But his strategy worked that time not because of top-down risk management—I was wrong, after all, and he was right—but because he acted as his own risk manager. Again, most people can't compete with the professionals—at least not over the long term. But by establishing long-term goals, and continually reevaluating your risk appetite, you can not only monitor the performance of the professionals into whose hands you have put your money, but help them help you to reach your goals.

This is true even though the investment business is no longer what it once was. The days of financial advisors buying shares of stock in specific companies, for instance, are long gone. Then, the investor would sit across from her broker at the end of each quarter and together they would review her portfolio's performance. If the majority of the stocks had gone up, the broker kept his job, and if the majority of the stocks had declined, the investor usually went looking for another broker. Today, brokers are far more likely to help you pick funds rather than individual stocks. Now, at the end of each quarter the broker sits on *your* side of the table and helps you evaluate the performance of the fund managers. If the broker understands your goals and your risk appetite—and respects them— then he selects funds that fit your profile. But that, of course, does not imply that the managers of the funds in which your broker invested your money have the same understanding of your goals, or your risk appetite, and therefore both you and your broker have to continue to be active risk managers. This means that you need to know not only your own risk appetite, but you need to know the amount of risk you're comfortable with *relative to the market*. Professionals call this beta risk, or the degree to which the risk of specific investments—in this case, the funds you and your broker have chosen—compare to the risks of the market as a whole.

While the control and management process just described is important, do not be misled into a false sense of security when there are only controls and no process.

Mechanical controls—including stop losses, performance pay hurdles, and high water marks—are good examples. While they are important tools for portfolio management, I prefer to think of them as speed bumps, or trip wires, rather than as substitutes for active risk management. They are meant not only to serve as decision-making mechanisms, but as warning signs to which you should respond. But most importantly, they are not a substitute for an embedded risk culture at the fund or fund complex where you have invested your assets.

Stop losses are triggered whenever prices sag beneath a certain level—typically a percentage of the overall value of each individual holding—and when they do your position is automatically sold. The specific stop loss percentage you choose is determined by a number of factors—for instance, stop losses on your other positions, the recent track record of your investments, and your overall risk appetite—but once established, it *dictates* your broker's actions. (It is worth noting in passing that the same sort of technique, used in reverse, governs some investors' *buying* strategies, not their *selling* strategies. In such cases, if the price of a stock falls below a certain predetermined level, the investor or her broker will *buy* the stock.)

Stop losses, however, just like every other risk management tool, can lead to both positive and negative outcomes. If your investments have achieved solid gains over the long term, stop losses are a useful mechanism for protecting those gains. For example, if you have realized a 20 percent return on an investment—that is, an investment of $100,000 has become $120,000—a 10 percent stop loss will ensure that you will still realize 8 percent of that gain ($120,000 less 10 percent, or $12,000, leaving you $108,000). Stop losses can also work against you, though, actually increasing your risk by limiting a position's chance for recovery in a volatile market. Over the years I have seen situations where the market opened 10 percent down, immediately triggering stop losses on various accounts. By the end of the day, however, the market had regained much of the ground it lost at the opening bell. The positions that were automatically closed out, therefore, could not benefit from the late surge. Volatility, then, must also be considered when bringing mechanical, or what might be called *automated* risk management mechanisms, to bear on your investments. Finally, while it clearly makes sense to *automatically* limit your losses, you probably shouldn't be in a particular game if the table limit is too high in relation to the stack of chips in front of you.

High water marks in hedge funds are another example of automated risk management mechanisms. Most hedge funds have a relatively simple payment arrangement, typically described as 2 and 20. The 2 refers to the 2 percent management fee of AUM at the beginning of each quarter. The 20 refers to the 20 percent *incentive* or *performance* fee due the manager on returns realized under certain conditions. High water marks set the level above which returns are subject to such incentive fees, and are based on each client's initial investment, which is *not adjusted lower* if the fund loses money. They can also include a *hurdle*—that is, an agreed upon minimum return, typically 5 percent—the manager must clear in order to receive incentive pay. A short example will help.

Let's say a hedge fund manager collects $10 million in assets from various investors and opens a new fund. To begin, she will be due 2 percent of AUM, as adjusted, each quarter. The first year the fund realizes a return of 30 percent, bringing AUM to $13 million. The hedge fund manager will be paid 20 percent of the *return over the 5 percent hurdle*, or $570,000 in incentive fees, in addition to the quarterly management fees of 2 percent of AUM. This leaves the fund with well over $12 million (presuming there are no redemptions), or a return of more than 20 percent on the initial investments. Everyone is happy.

The following year, however, the fund loses 25 percent, leaving less than $9 million in AUM once the quarterly management fees have been assessed. This means investors have lost more than 10 percent of their *initial* investments, and that the fund manager will receive no incentive pay. No one is happy.

Now the fund manager must realize truly astounding returns— that is, in excess of 30 percent, in order to clear both the high water mark and the hurdle—the following year, or she will receive *no incentive fees for the second year in a row*. At that point she may decide to close the fund, because the automated risk management mechanism will make it almost impossible for her to earn any incentive fees—and more importantly, for you to recoup your losses. The point is that depending on a variety of risk management tools and controls, instead of a culture of risk management, can sometimes *defeat* you and your long-term strategies.

What, then, can you do as an investor? Or put another way, what are the tell-tale signs you should monitor?

The answer leads us back to transparency, which I discussed in Risk Principle 4. When performance statements are not delivered on time, or requests for withdrawal are not immediately accommodated, even investors managing their assets from afar should hear a fire alarm ringing loudly. Another tell-tale indicator is frequent personnel charges. Finally, if *at any time* your financial advisors cannot clearly explain how they generate alpha—that is, returns in excess of the risks of your investments—you should immediately take steps to protect your assets. And once again, if your advisors insist that their methods are beyond your understanding, refer them to Einstein, who wrote, referring to the work of the mathematician Minkowski:

> Minkowski's work is doubtless difficult of access to anyone inexperienced in mathematics, but . . . *it is not necessary to have a very exact grasp of this work in order to understand the fundamental ideas* [my italics] of either the special or the general theory of relativity. . . .

In other words, if Einstein could make his theories understandable to a lay audience—scientifically speaking—even though they had an imperfect understanding of certain critical mathematical models—your investment advisors should be able to explain their methods to you.

Even if it is impossible to track daily activity in an investment fund, I personally take note if a fund manager I know seems to be too busy with a new toy, instead of focusing on what's going on in the office. This happens quite frequently when someone earns a great deal of money very quickly. That toy might be a yacht, a Broadway play in which she's invested, or even another investment vehicle, any of which would make me wonder if the manager is still focused on her job. As I've said before, and will continue to repeat at every opportunity, good risk management requires hard work—on your part and on the part of those working for you. Get everyone involved, but you have to stay involved yourself.

The ready availability of prices is another sign of sound risk management, and the absence of such prices is a clear warning signal. Are the prices of your holdings marked-to-market every day? If so, who prices them? Are they priced by the market or by the firm that handles them, and if the latter, are the prices independently checked? Also, how do your managers value illiquid securities? Finally, it is equally important to understand the total expenses of any fund. If they are excessive—that is, higher than industry standards—you are automatically incurring greater risk.

When a manager has multiple funds—something quite common in the industry—I naturally worry about conflicts of interest. The way trades are allocated between funds, for instance, can make a huge difference in fund performance. I recall a situation where an asset manager set up a legal structure known as a *master feeder*, ostensibly to save money every time he opened up a new fund. When I examined his documents, however, I realized that the walls separating the various funds and strategies were somewhat porous, and that if one fund failed, the losses could bleed into another. A lay person may have great difficulty reading through fund documents to discover such an arrangement, but remember Einstein and Minkowski. At the very least, you should familiarize yourself with the risk section of the fund documents, and if you can't understand the general risks you are undertaking by investing in the fund, ask for clarification— and don't stop asking until you are satisfied with the answer. If the returns are sufficient to warrant it, you might also pay an expert to demystify the arrangement. And if you can't, you should choose a less sophisticated investment vehicle.

Some investors require more transparency than others, depending on the investment. If I invest in currencies, I know better than to expect to walk into an office and see euros, yen, yuan, and dollars in a corner safe. If I invest in real estate, however, I want to be able to drive by and see it.

Finally, while risk management should be practiced from top to bottom in any organization, it is equally important that every investment firm has an independent risk manager who reports *directly* to the fund's senior leadership. You can also think of this as a *challenge* function within the organization. Large institutional investors, for instance, insist on meeting both the asset manager and the risk manager, and pepper both with questions from standardized checklists. They are curious to know how both approach the potential for operational errors, what rules exist for large positions, how the firm measures liquidity risk, how counterparties are approved, and whether or not the firm has a disaster recovery plan. It's one thing if a power outage takes out the grid on the entire Eastern Seaboard, and another altogether if everyone else has power, is still doing business, and only your lights are out.

Finally, the open discussion of risk shouldn't be confined to your investment advisor's office or your company's Chief Risk Officer. Your accountant should be a part of the discussion, too, and so should your lawyer. Even more importantly, everyone in your immediate family—or in other words, all of those who will be affected by the results of your investment strategies—should be kept in the loop.

A Story of Risk: Part 9

The biopsy of Max's duodenum confirmed the gastroenterologist's diagnosis. The tumor was malignant. The question now became how to treat the disease, where it should be done, and who should do it.

There wasn't much time. The tumor, presumably, was growing with every passing day, and although it was still in an early stage, and appeared not to have spread to surrounding lymph nodes or other major organs, if it reached a certain stage surgery might no longer be feasible. But Max, although he heard the clock ticking, was determined to learn as much as he could about the disease and its treatment before making a decision.

The biopsy had been done at a local hospital, and although the surgeons there were capable of doing either of the most frequently recommended surgeries, they were not specialists. Determined to get the best care possible, Max spent hours on his computer searching for the most experienced doctors in the field, and just as importantly, the best facilities. Once he had made his decision, and his wife had confirmed that the practice accepted their insurance, he took the next available appointment with a specialist at the facility.

The surgeon, who had performed the procedure hundreds of times, would not see Max again until the day of the surgery. But his staff was already hard at work. After Max and Barbara shook hands with the surgeon, they were taken to see the office manager, who gave them the appropriate paperwork along with detailed instructions on how to complete it. The following day, Max and Barbara met with a nurse practitioner who had worked in the field for more than two decades. She walked them through every step of the process, letting them know how Max, and his family, should prepare for the surgery, and what they could expect after its conclusion. He would be in intensive care for several days, and would remain in the hospital for as long as two weeks. When he returned home, he would be cared for by a visiting nurse, and if necessary, a housekeeper could be assigned to help Barbara while she was caring for Max. If Max and Barbara thought it would be helpful, the entire family could meet with one of the staff psychologists so they could prepare themselves for the inevitable difficulties.

Once Max's incisions had healed, and the biopsy results were in, he would next meet with one of the oncologists on staff to determine his subsequent treatment. Once that treatment had begun, she strongly recommended that Max meet with one of the staff psychiatrists, since depression was a common aftereffect of life-threatening surgery, and if left untreated might delay Max's recovery. Before they left, she gave him a series of phone numbers that either he or his wife could call at any time of the day or night. It was important for him to know, she said, that everyone in the organization was now working together to treat his illness.

Rob had already slipped into a routine at his new job, and while building a client base was a lot more work than he thought it would be, at least it kept Lisa off his back. He did, however, often find himself thinking of the good old days back at the bank. There, all he had to do was bring clients in through the front door; as a stock broker, he not only had to find clients, *he had to* come up with investment plans. And once he'd completed his training, there was no one to turn to for help. During the company's regular meetings the brass spent a lot of time talking about working together, but the moment those meetings broke up, it was everyone for himself. Hot stock picks were concealed, as was any inside information, and whenever a broker lost his job because he couldn't generate sufficient sales, a free-for-all ensued as the other brokers went after his clients.

At home Rob was about as much help as his coworkers were at the brokerage. Lisa was doing her best to follow her OB/GYN's instructions, but the first thing Rob did when he got home was pour himself a drink, and her a small glass of wine. She didn't want him to drink by himself, did she? Their diet didn't exactly follow the prenatal care textbook either. Lisa was too tired to cook, and Rob didn't know how, so they ate a lot of takeout.

Risk Principle | 10

THE IMPORTANCE
OF REPUTATION

*"Many a man's reputation would not know his character
if they met on the street."*
—Elbert Hubbard

We are born with our hands closed. We die with our hands open. We are born, in other words, attempting to grasp our needs and our wants, and we reach for them as long as we live. Since we can take nothing with us at death, however, we die with our hands open, as if we have finally let go of everything we sought in life.

While this belief has shifted over the centuries—think of the ancient Egyptians, who included provisions for the afterlife with their dead—few today would argue that our material possessions, the very things we spend the greater part of our lives trying to accumulate, are of little use to us when we pass out of this world.

Spiritual possessions, on the other hand—at least according to some religious beliefs—can survive death. Think of the Hindu belief in reincarnation, where enlightened beings seek ever higher levels of understanding, and are reborn again and again until they reach divine form. The Talmud contains a slightly more worldly example, asserting that the central goal of life is to achieve a good name—and that a person can take their good name with them to the grave.

Whether or not your good name survives you, there is little doubt that your reputation, and the reputations of those with whom you do business, should figure in the decisions you make regarding your relationships, your finances, your business—or, in short, your life. It takes years to build a good reputation, but only a few minutes to destroy one—a reality that too few people seem to understand, or understand only after they have squandered their good names. Whether or not it survives you, a good reputation has a distinct value in this life, and casually sacrificing it, or failing to consider the reputations of those with whom you do business, constitutes poor risk management in and of itself.

Before going any farther, we should also consider the relationship between reputation and transparency: Transparency reveals *how* business is done, while reputation reveals *who* you're doing business with. Flip sides of the same coin, both are necessary to effectively de-risk your plans.

To better understand this, it may also help to look at the difference between moral and legal decisions, the former of which are far more nuanced than the latter. If, for instance, you coast through a red light at 3:00 in the morning, you are without a doubt *legally* guilty of breaking the law, but most of us would not feel *morally* culpable. The law is designed to reduce the risk of automobile accidents, and at that hour of the night there are few automobiles on the road. If you coasted through the red light during rush hour, however, greatly increasing the risk of an accident because of the heavy traffic, you would be breaking both the statutory law *and* the moral law that prohibits us from doing harm to others. If, finally, you *ran* the red light, you would be both legally and morally guilty at any hour of the day or night. Again, few of your acquaintances would judge you harshly for rolling through the light at 3:00 in the morning, but almost all of them would if you did the same thing during rush hour. And yet, as thick as the line is between being reasonably respectful of the rules, and in perfect compliance with the law, many people are still unable to see it.

To take a more concrete example, we all understand that our financial holdings will rise and fall over time. This is a short-term risk that all investors accept, because it is dependent on the markets, which no one can control. If, however, you invest your money in a hedge fund, and an *operational error* on the part of the fund leads to a loss in your account, you will naturally expect them to make you whole. The error was management's, and therefore the remedy is their responsibility as well. And by doing so, they not only satisfy their legal and moral responsibilities, but maintain their good reputation.

Despite the hundreds of millions of dollars spent every year to promote motion pictures, both those who buy tickets and those in the business know that a blockbuster lives or dies on word of mouth. The same thing is true of books. Your eyes might happen across an ad in a newspaper, and even pause for a moment while you study the photograph of the author. But that alone won't cause you to read the book. If, however, a friend of yours can't stop talking about the book, you're all but certain to find yourself a copy.

Reputation is built in the same manner—by word of mouth. Consider the following examples, and ask yourself with which of these money managers you'd like to do business.

1. Ten million dollars sits idle for nearly six months as the result of a clerical mistake. The funds, intended for an equity account, ended up in a money market account instead. The customer received monthly statements, and between the time she sat down with her advisor at the beginning of the year, and the time the error was eventually discovered, she never spotted the mistake. When it was finally pointed out to her, she wondered whether there was a statute of limitations on such cases. When she spoke to her broker, he asked for a day or two to check into the details. At their next meeting, he informed her that the company would make up the difference between the return on the equity and money market accounts over that period—an amount in excess of $200,000—and apologized for not having caught the error himself.

2. A trading error occurred which resulted in a $2 million gain in a client's account. The client was allowed to keep the gain but was charged $20,000 in transaction costs.

3. A client opened an international account, and equity trades began at the approximate start date. The foreign exchange conversion, however—that is, the conversion of the client's dollars into euros—was not done until T+4 (trade date plus four days), leading to overdraft charges in the client's account. The overdraft charges, once the client discovered them, were credited to the client's account, but the conversion was recorded using the current exchange rate in effect four days after the

trade was made, leading to a small gain. (The value of the dollar had increased against the euro during that time.)

In the first example, there is little doubt that the customer is entitled to the difference in the return on the two accounts. The error was the company's, not hers, and as the error led to a significant loss, the company was required—both by law, and by any reasonable moral standard—to make the client whole. The company's reputation was made, however—at least for this particular client—by the manner in which restitution was made. As soon as the error was brought to the broker's attention, he calculated the gain she would have achieved had her wishes been followed and immediately credited her account, without any attempt at negotiation or recrimination, even though the client had missed the error for six months.

The second example is less clear cut. The error, once again, was the company's, but in this case the client profited from it. Should the advisor, then, be allowed to recover the transaction costs that led to the gain? A reputable firm would raise the issue—the company is in business, after all, to make money—but would leave its resolution to the client's discretion.

The third case is even more subtle. While the overdraft charges occurred as the result of an operational error, and therefore clearly should have been credited to the client's account—that is, the company should not have begun trading in the account until the client's assets had been converted into the appropriate currency—the fortuitous gain on the foreign exchange is somewhat problematical. While the investment advisor is not *required* to unjustly enrich any client, given that the currency exchange error was made on the part of the advisor, he would be wise to pass along the full benefit of the gain on the foreign exchange. By forgoing the small gain, he establishes a high standard of care, and adds to his firm's reputation.

The above examples can be resolved by appealing both to commonsense and industry standards, but reputations are often made or lost as a result of circumstances that are not quite as black and white. When I was a boy, I knew a man in our neighborhood—a very religious man—who was about to close his business for two working days in order to observe a religious holiday. Just before he shut his doors, a longtime customer called and placed an order. The business owner shipped the merchandise the same night, and absorbed the cost of a one-day delivery. Two days later, shortly after reopening his business, the customer called the store owner to thank him for the timely delivery, saying: "I knew the holidays were coming up, and I never expected you to pay extra so I could receive the merchandise on time." As pleased as he was to hear this, the store owner responded: "Who said I have to make money on every transaction?" It was this "clients first" mentality that endeared the store owner to his customers, and secured his good reputation.

This same mentality on the customer's side, as we all know, is far from universal. In fact, in recent years we have seen an ocean of credit card debt run up by those who appear to think that if the day comes when they can't make their payments they'll just declare bankruptcy and wipe their slates clean. Unfortunately—both for them and the institutions that lent them money—they don't understand that bankruptcy will affect their ability to get a school loan, a mortgage, or a small business loan—that is, to enjoy the benefits of credit—for at least seven years. And even after that lengthy period has passed, these casual bankrupts will have difficulty establishing new lines of credit. In this case, the persons involved may have satisfied their legal obligations by filing for bankruptcy protection according to the rule of law, but in so doing they may have violated moral law by refusing to acknowledge their obligations. The same thing is true of those who overstated their incomes when applying for mortgages. Yes, the originator of the mortgage took a risk by not verifying their income, but by joining the deception, the applicants surrendered their moral right to object to foreclosure once they were unable to make their monthly payments. The point is, once again, that you should carefully consider all risks to your reputation before making any financial decisions, including everything from long-term loans to spur-of-the-moment purchases motivated by the availability of credit, rather than your ability to pay.

Those who work for you can also affect your reputation—if they fail, it's your reputation that suffers. Therefore, you need to do due diligence on the people who do business *for* you, as well as those you do business with—and you must do this due diligence *before* you put them to work *in your name*. You may be surprised at what you find, but be quite pleased to have found it before you sign their first paycheck. As for those with whom you are considering doing business, a simple Dun & Bradstreet background check, which costs only $25, is an exceptionally small price to pay for an enormous amount of peace of mind.

Reputations are lost every day. A brief review of the newspapers over the past few years will show you multi-millionaires who have cheated their home contractors, their beauticians, and even those who have cared for their children. The same newspapers contain numerous accounts of political appointees who have failed their confirmation hearings because of neglected tax returns, household help without green cards, or business connections with persons who have run afoul of the law.

The case of the Reserve Primary Fund, a money market fund which "broke the buck" in 2008—that is, was unable to maintain the value of each of its shares at $1—is an excellent example of the value of reputation, and the irreparable costs connected to its loss. At the time, Reserve Primary was one of the oldest money market funds in the nation, and as such had long advocated the sort of conservative investment strategies designed to make money market funds the safest investment available—that is, as nearly equivalent to cash as possible, while still paying a small return. To do so the fund typically invested the bulk of its assets in exceptionally safe instruments like certificates of deposit, U.S. Treasury bills, U.S. government obligations, and to a lesser extent, reasonably safe investments like commercial paper. Reserve Primary, like all money market funds, was regulated by the Securities and Exchange Commission (SEC), and was required to hold debt that matured within 13 months or less (with a weighted average maturity of no more than 90 days). This debt was also required by law to have top-notch short-term corporate debt ratings.

Approximately one week after Lehman Brothers collapsed, Reserve Primary was forced to write off almost $800 million of debt issued by Lehman Brothers—that is, to admit that it was worthless. Subsequent reports suggested that while the fund's management professed to follow conservative investment strategies, they had in fact begun to invest in riskier debt in order to offer higher returns, and attract more assets. The Lehman Brothers commercial paper, in fact, had become high-risk debt long before it had to be written off, and was therefore an inappropriate—and some might say an *illegal*—investment given SEC regulations.

Although the amount written off was not much more than 1 percent of fund's AUM, which then totaled more than $60 billion, the write-off caused the share price to drop 3 *cents* below one dollar. Redemptions were suspended temporarily, but only after some institutional investors had been able to withdraw their assets at full value. Approximately one week later, when redemptions were allowed to continue, anxious investors withdrew their assets, effectively closing the fund and ending any possibility that they could recoup their losses. In the meantime, the U.S. government was forced to provide temporary FDIC coverage of all money market funds in order to keep investors from withdrawing their assets, and in so doing essentially closing the market for short-term commercial paper. Litigation continues today, but the once-proud name of Reserve Money Management does not.

Again, I am reminded of events that took place after I left Citibank and opened my own hedge fund. Until I left, I didn't realize that I worked in a protective cocoon, so to speak, and was never exposed to the underbelly of Wall Street. Shortly after I opened my own business, however, I was introduced to a so-called Rothschild, a man who looked and acted the part. Despite my desire to attract capital, I asked my lawyer to run a simple background search on him and was quickly informed that he was an imposter with a checkered past. His reputation did not withstand scrutiny, but mine survived.

That reputation continued to serve me when I went to work for AllianceBernstein. When management decided to divest itself of the company's Private Equity Group, I was given the job of handling the negotiations. Both the company and the individual investors knew my reputation, and as a result I was able to resolve the difficult issues surrounding the divestiture without either side questioning my motives. My reputation took years to create, but it continually pays dividends.

Walter Wriston was able to take the same high road during one particularly difficult situation at Citibank. The story involved one of two large clients who wanted to undertake a hostile takeover of other and wished to borrow money from Citibank to do it. At the time the request came, Wriston was out of the office, and bank management was frozen in the face of this seemingly irresolvable quandary. To loan the money to one would surely alienate the other. Wriston, once back in the office, did not hesitate. Lending money is what we do, he said. We're a common carrier, like a railroad, and anyone who has a ticket can ride. Within a short time the loan was approved, and while feelings ran high, Citibank's reputation for integrity was preserved.

A few years later I attended a training session conducted by a couple of former CIA agents. I attended the session because I wanted to get a better sense of when a company's management was shading the truth. During the course, the agents made a few changes in the layout of the conference room. The carpets were removed so that our chairs could roll more easily, and the wood conference table was exchanged for one with a glass top. The ex-CIA agents told us to watch for people moving their hands or feet, or rolling their chairs a bit when they began to answer questions. These were subtle but powerful signs that the person answering the questions was uncomfortable, and while not necessarily lying, was perhaps not telling the "whole" truth. Based on that experience, AllianceBernstein made similar changes in their conference rooms so that we could take advantage of similar "tells" when we met with those with whom we did business.

Over the years, I have also noticed that those people who take seats directly opposite you, instead of sitting on the same side as you, tend to be more contentious. I would not go so far as to say that they are arranging themselves as an enemy might, but I do tend to be more cautious when I encounter such behavior. I have also found that those people who shake your hand, it seems, with their entire body, and look you in the eye as they do so, tend to be more sincere than those who do not. These are all small things, taken one at a time, but together they create what we call "reputation," and a wise risk manager will take note of them.

To conclude, let's consider the example of one man whose reputation has survived every one of the market crises described in this book—from the oil embargo of the early 1970s through the decade of stagflation that followed it, from the savings and loan crisis of the late 1980s through the dotcom boom and bust, and finally, through the speculative bubble of the first decade of the twenty-first century through the financial crisis of 2007–2009. That man, of course, is Warren Buffett.

Over the last 40-plus years, despite a series of steadily escalating shocks to U.S. and global markets, Buffett's Berkshire Hathaway has produced annual compounded gains *in excess of 20 percent*. The success of Buffett's company is the result of value investing, a relatively simple but labor-intensive approach predicated on the following principles: Buy companies that you know and understand; buy companies with good long-term prospects; buy companies with honest and competent management; and buy companies that are selling at attractive prices (i.e., relative to their true value). Contrast this approach with the frequently quoted comment by Charles Prince in July 2007, when he was CEO of Citibank, regarding his company's inability to ignore the short-term opportunities for profit from the housing bubble that would burst just a few months later:

> When the music stops, in terms of liquidity, things will be complicated. But as long as the music is playing, you've got to get up and dance. We're still dancing.

Buffett, quite simply, never danced to that music, and as a result his shareholders missed out on some of the market's great upswings—in particular, the dotcom boom, which he admitted he did not understand, and the early years of the recent asset bubble. When Prince's music stopped playing, however, Buffett was able to keep dancing, because he had been dancing to a different song all along. As a result, even during the leaner years—and there have been very few of them—Berkshire Hathaway's investors remained loyal, because Buffett's reputation was unassailable.

A Story of Risk: Part 10

Three months later, with both the surgery and the initial period of recovery behind him, Max was back in the office waiting to see his oncologist. His prognosis, at least, was good. All of the biopsies taken during the surgery had been negative, demonstrating that the cancer had not spread to any of the surrounding tissues, but he was far from out of the woods. The five-year survival rate, even for early-stage victims like himself, was not good. But it was enough to look at the faces of many of the patients and families sitting around him to know that he had been far luckier than most of them.

When he had finished reading the business section of the *Wall Street Journal* he turned to the man sitting next to him and asked if he'd like to take a look. The man shook his head. He'd been waiting for almost two hours and had already read the paper from front to back. As they both sat there, however, they began to talk. The man, who was about ten years older than Max, had undergone the same procedure Max had. His prognosis, too, was good, and they both agreed that they had been extraordinarily lucky. Had they contracted their illnesses 25 years earlier, they probably would not have survived.

As it happened the man was a banker, and before long he and Max were talking business. When his name was called the man got up, wished Max the best of luck, and then gave him his business card. He hadn't returned to work full-time yet, so if Max liked, perhaps the two of them could get together for lunch sometime soon.

They met the following week, and by the time they'd finished their meal the banker had offered Max a job. Certainly their shared brush with death had had something to do with the offer, but it turned out there was more behind it. Max, despite being bowled over by the offer of employment, nonetheless felt it necessary to bring up the events that led to his leaving his last job. He didn't get far. Before he was halfway through the story the banker put up a hand to stop him, and then told Max that he had already spoken to several people in the accounting firm, including Max's former boss. But he hadn't stopped there. He had made additional inquiries, and had quickly discovered the truth. In fact, the negative job review from Max's ex-boss—whose reputation was far from spotless—had cinched the deal. The banker had friends in the accounting world too, and once he heard from them that Max's boss couldn't be trusted, he knew that Max could.

It was no small blessing that the markets had begun to soar again almost as soon as Rob had become a stock broker, because he quickly developed a reputation for being hard to reach once he'd convinced a new client to put their assets in his hands. He didn't let the occasional gripes bother him though—if his clients wanted to know what was going on, they could always turn to the back pages of the *Wall Street Journal*. In the meantime, he needed every commission he could generate if he was going to be able to pay the bills himself once Lisa stopped working. And given her age, the difficult nature of her pregnancy, and her doctor's advice, she wouldn't be taking the subway downtown much longer.

Risk Principle | 11

FIT YOUR DECISION MAKING INTO SPECIFIC TIME FRAMES

"If a person is interested in one year, plant wheat.
If a person is interested in a decade, build buildings.
If a person is interested in eternity, have children."
—The Talmud

When my father died, I lost an important piece of myself, but I couldn't tell anyone exactly what was missing, because I didn't know myself. So I went on with my life, and when the initial shock had finally passed, I began to return to the rhythm I had followed when he was still alive. My family and my work sustained me, but I was never able to shake the feeling that something was missing, something vital, and no matter how hard I tried, I was never able to put my finger on it.

Months went by, and the feeling persisted, and every once in a while I would find myself alone in my car at night, and I would hear a song, or I would see something that reminded me of my father, and I would begin to cry. I cried for my father, of course, whom I had loved, but I also cried for that missing piece of myself—a piece, I began to think, that would never be replaced, that I would have to go through life without.

Those feelings continue to well up in me to this day, and I suspect, and even hope, that they will continue to surface for the rest of my life. I was made whole again, however, only when my eldest son had a child, and named him after my father. Only then did I realize that I could not replace the piece of me I had lost when my father died—that piece could be replaced only by the first member of my family's next generation.

Time and humanity's continual regeneration combined to dull the pain of my emotional loss. In financial matters, however, time can either heal a wound or make it deeper—time, in other words, magnifies both positive and negative events in a dramatic way. Therefore, your plans must be made within specific time frames, and to the extent possible you should remain committed to them. That said, as your personal circumstances change, your goals change, and economic conditions change, you will often have to make new decisions. And whether or not circumstances allow you to respect your earlier time frame, as you change your plans you should always do so with a specific interval in mind.

First, let's consider the effect of time on negative results—or on decisions that failed to work out. If, for purposes of illustration, the value of your portfolio on January 1, 2008, was $1,000,000, a 25 percent loss over 12 months would leave you with $750,000. (For this example, we will not consider dividends, interest, or inflation, simply the loss of principal.) As painful as such a result is by itself, it's far worse when you realize that you'll need a return of 33 percent—on the remaining $750,000—just to *recover* your loss. In other words, even if your portfolio grew by approximately 10 percent every year that followed—a rate at which few would sneer—it would not regain the value it had on January 1, 2008, *for almost three years!* Making good decisions, then, with specific time frames in mind, means weighing the potentially negative results of those decisions as well, and the time that may be necessary to put them back on track.

This, however, does not necessarily mean bailing out as soon as things go wrong, as recent events in the markets demonstrate. If, on October 1, 2007, the domestic equities portion of your 410(k) portfolio was worth $1 million and was invested in an index that tracked the Dow Jones Industrial Average (DJIA), by March 1, 2009, the value of those assets would have declined by approximately $500,000, or 50 percent. But if, having watched the steady, heartbreaking decline of the value of your holdings for almost a year and a half, you could no longer bear the emotional risk of further losses, and abandoned your position, you would have *locked in* the second largest percentage loss—over that time frame—in the history of the U.S. stock market. As most readers know, you would also have missed the market rebound that followed, which would have restored your portfolio to more than 75 percent of its value a few years earlier. Not good news, a 25 percent loss over two years, but far better than a 50 percent loss—to say nothing of the emotional scar you would bear for years afterward, knowing that you had made precisely the wrong decision.

What's more, this scenario—which admittedly does not take into account the value of your other, presumably well-diversified assets—

would have been almost impossible had you respected the time frame you set for your investments, instead of reacting to swings, however large, in the market. That $1 million on October 1, 2007, after all, had been worth only about $500,000 *five years earlier.*

Time is far kinder, as you will see below, to small gains than it is to large losses. Take, for example, an equity portfolio that gained 9 percent every year. In such a case your principal—again, without taking into account interest, dividends, and inflation—would double every seven years. Therefore, if your portfolio was worth $1 million when you were 40 years old, and you enjoyed two decades of 9 percent annual returns, it's value would rise to more than $4 million. Of course anyone familiar with the markets knows that such returns—that is, such steady returns—are all but impossible, and yet twice in the last 70 years, from 1942 to 1962, and from 1982 to 2002, your returns would have *far exceeded* the 9 percent scenario. It is only fair to note, though, that had you chosen to invest your money from 1962 to 1982 in U.S. equities, your returns would have been far, far smaller. And if you took inflation into account, you would have *lost* money, in terms of buying power, that is.

We should also note that the 9 percent scenario I've used to make this point was perfectly *un*-diversified, invested only in an index fund that tracked the DJIA. If your portfolio had included foreign equities as well, along with domestic and foreign bonds, as well as some currency positions and perhaps a real estate component, your returns would have been more moderate during the booms, but less affected by the busts. Finally, the scenario I used was based on a *passive*, rather than a dynamic, approach to investing. By selecting *certain* stocks and bonds your returns would have been vastly different—both better and worse—but the permutations are far too numerous to attempt here.

Besides, this is not a book for stock pickers—it is a review of the principles of risk management, which taken together can be used to create a framework for decision making. Toward that end, the time frame is critical. In a certain way, it can be considered the structure within which initial investment, additional inflows, varying outflows, and of course the rate of return, work to create gains. Put another way, it provides the period within which principal and any additional funding is multiplied by the rate of return, compounded during the length of the investment. For this reason, since the greatest impact on compounded growth will occur during the portfolio's earliest years—when losses might set the fund back for years, and gains might position it for even better long-term gains— a younger investor might consider a more conservative approach when beginning to invest, confident that over time a sound strategy will eventually produce solid returns.

Foreshortened Time Frames

Retirement planning requires a different calculation—one dependent on a foreshortened time frame, within which returns and withdrawals must be carefully balanced. In essence, a retiree in the final third of her life has had her time frame chosen for her, but as life expectancy is highly variable, decisions must still be made as time *passes.* This is also true for companies, which change their strategies as their services or products mature, taking into account industry and/or business cycles—stages much like the ones individuals pass through over the course of their lives. Seen this way, it is obviously more important for a company in its startup phase to assess cyclical risks in conjunction with financing requirements and projected revenues.

For an individual in retirement, though, at the end of their personal "business cycle," it is important to understand that there is no difference in return whether your investments lose value because of fluctuations in the market, or whether you withdraw principal to support your lifestyle. Again, performance is equal to principal, multiplied by return, multiplied by time, and so no matter how or why the principal rises or falls, the effect is the same on your holdings. This is true for younger investors as well, but they add one critical factor to the equation—earned income. The absence of that inflow—which may allow a younger investor to leave principal intact as it compounds over the years—makes lifestyle costs a far more important consideration for retirees.

Determining "core" lifestyle costs, then, is the most critical part of retirement planning. If—or once—those costs can be covered, then the discussion turns to discretionary spending—for instance, gifts to family, charitable giving, or additional investments. Not all retirees, of course, will have to worry about meeting core lifestyle costs, but for those who do, the key variable is their rate of spending relative to their retirement portfolio's *projected* returns. Finally, they must take into account the variable and unpredictable effects of taxation—which can be mitigated by tax-deferred or tax-free investments—as well as the effects of inflation and longevity. This last is a critical consideration, and may force a 65-year-old to make spending decisions an 85-year-old need not.

Once core lifestyle costs have been determined—even though these may well change over time if, for instance, a retiree changes his principal place of residence—the focus shifts to investment strategy. For the purposes of the following discussion I will presume that our hypothetical retiree depends on the return from his investment to meet his core lifestyle needs—or in other words, that the return on his investments will affect his ability to spend at a given rate over the remainder of his life.

Common retirement scenarios *presume* a somewhat conservative approach, given the disappearance of earned income, but depending on an individual's goals, that may not always be the case. Those, for instance, who wish to leave a substantial portion of their portfolios to their heirs, may have to seek higher returns, or to constrain spending, while those who simply wish to live out their days at a certain level of comfort may be able to draw on their principal over time without endangering their lifestyles. The latter would likely be more comfortable with fixed-income investments, while the former may have to put some portion of their assets at risk in order to generate higher returns. The success of either plan, however, will almost certainly be affected by inflation and taxation, and so even those with conservative goals would do well to add a certain percentage of equities to their retirement portfolios. This is especially true because retirees, unlike investors still in the workforce, are often unable to make additional contributions to compensate for short-term losses. (Even retirees, though, should consider the possibility that an inheritance, or the sale of existing assets, like real estate, may occasionally allow them to add to their retirement portfolios.) No matter their approach to investing, however, or the length of their time frame, even retired investors still need to continually monitor their needs, wants, and returns, and to be prepared to make changes in their plans when necessary.

As I've noted earlier, nearly everyone, whether poor or rich, young or old, has one essential goal—to maintain their present lifestyle, or put another way, to avoid being worse off as the years go by. For those with shortened investment time frames, that desire is especially strong, and as a result investment decisions are especially stressful. That stress cannot be eliminated, but it can be managed—managed so that a life of hard work does not end in disappointment, but instead offers new opportunities for personal enrichment. I should add, in passing, given the global demographic data I discussed earlier, that the individuals making these sorts of decisions are going to have a lot of company. By 2029, the last of the baby boomers will be 65-years-old, and shortly thereafter she will join the more than 77 million persons born between 1946 and 1964 who have gone into retirement. And that mass exodus from the workforce will have a significant impact on social services spending, health-care costs, taxation, and inflation, the last of which will affect the *buying power* of your assets, and therefore core spending.

Having decided how much you'll need, in today's dollars, to support your lifestyle, you must then make some sort of prediction regarding your longevity. The overall state of your health and your family's medical history will provide you with some clues, but in general everyone is living longer. Women in particular. This may be due to diet, lifestyle, or personal wealth, but there is little doubt that advances in medicine, especially in treating diseases that were once remorseless killers—like heart disease and cancer—have also greatly prolonged life. And they will most likely continue to do so. So a person retiring in 2010 at the age of 65, expecting to live at least another 15 years, will almost certainly see further advances in medicine during those years, and therefore will most likely live even longer. This means that when setting time frames, retirees clearly should err on the side of optimism. If, for instance, you create a spending plan that covers all reasonable contingencies for the next 15 years, and live instead for another 25 years, you will almost certainly find it difficult to maintain your lifestyle. And if during those additional ten years you suffer some sort of debilitating illness, the costs of care may actually wipe out your savings. Healthcare insurance, therefore, and perhaps even some sort of extended care policy, are vital parts of any retirement plan.

And keep in mind that as those years pass, whether there are 15 or 25 of them, the costs of goods and services will rise continually, requiring higher spending simply to maintain your lifestyle. It's true, predicting the rate of inflation is something like predicting the direction of the markets, but even moderate inflation over the course of two decades—say, approximately 3 percent—will cut your *buying power in half*—or, in other words, will make it necessary to double your budget in order to maintain your lifestyle. And should the rate of inflation over those two decades be higher still—say, approximately 6 percent—your budget will have to nearly quadruple in order for you to live in the manner to which you have become accustomed. I'll leave it to each individual reader to guess what the rate of inflation will actually be over the course of their retirement, but given current levels of federal spending, and demographic trends that promise a smaller workforce—and thus competition for workers' services in the form of wages—readers are unlikely to be disappointed if they prepare for a worst-case scenario. And as long as we're looking ahead, keep in mind that increases in the cost of health care have surpassed the rate of inflation for more than—well, for as long as records have been kept. And while your financial circumstances may allow you to absorb these higher costs, you will either have to cut back on other expenses, increase the amount of money you draw from your retirement account annually, or adopt a somewhat more aggressive investment strategy hoping to make up the difference. Finally, while Medicare may not be a part of *your* health-care strategy, ask yourself how many of the 77 million retiring baby boomers will tap its benefits, and what that nearly incalculable cost will mean to future rates of taxation.

Inflationary pressures, then, along with core lifestyle costs, must be considered within your time frame, and if that time frame extends past your working years, remember that you will be deprived of one of the few forces that effectively combats inflation—that is, rising wages. Taken together, these factors will naturally bear on your allocation strategy—or more accurately, your risk appetite. And to conclude the sobering discussion of the effect of inflation on spending needs, if your plans include providing for the higher education of your grandchildren, you would do well to consider that while the cost of living has trebled over the past 30 years, and the costs of medical care has risen sixfold, the cost of a private college degree has risen *tenfold*.

Taken together, then, the calculation of spending needs and inflationary pressures makes a conservative approach to investing during the retirement time frame seem decidedly short-sighted— and one more example, you might say, of the need to know what you don't know. And even if you have been successful enough, or fortunate enough, to cover your core lifestyle needs in spite of costs that are all but certain to rise, your discretionary spending should be considered in the same light. If, for instance, you wish to leave a substantial legacy, or simply to *maintain* your charitable giving, your risk appetite must be adjusted to cover your goals.

The liquidity of your holdings is also a critical consideration. At the age of 50, with an established career and income that is still rising, emergency expenditures or fluctuations in the markets can be offset by lowering your contributions to retirement or college education plans, or by reducing your charitable giving. Similar emergencies at the age of 70—whether related to your physical health, or your financial health—can be met only by tapping your assets. Therefore, while your long-term plans may include less liquid investments that will produce higher returns, you should also consider the possibility that circumstances may make it necessary for you to make unanticipated withdrawals from your holdings, and to allocate your resources accordingly.

Seen in this light, sound decision making involves the consideration not only of the short-term, *immediate* effects of risk—including the present economic environment and the nature of the investments themselves—but the long-term factors as well, especially when your time frame is foreshortened. This appears obvious, but since we're all too easily seduced by our desire for immediate gratification, we often ignore the long-term implications of our decisions. Moreover, in the absence of forethought, time has a way of making decisions for us. To prevent that, you need to think about the long haul, considering different time parameters and how you can reach your goals within them. Clearly, if you want to retire within three to five years, your investing strategies should be far different than if you're planning to retire in 30 years.

One way to do this is to reflect not only on who you are but who you want to *become*. The easiest path in life—but the one least likely to lead to success—is to continue doing what you're already doing. The future, however, is not the present pushed forward, and continually reevaluating your goals through the inevitable changes of life requires self-reflection and innovation. Successful decision making requires a critical look at ourselves and our plans, considering not only what we want, but also what is happening around us, then determining how best to navigate those circumstances, and making our decisions accordingly.

To return again to retirement planning, the retiree's personal hierarchy of needs gives an initial shape to the appropriate retirement strategy. This hierarchy starts with lifestyle, and requires a cold, hard look at normal spending patterns, the amount of money one should set aside for emergencies—which we can consider "core" needs—and then progresses to discretionary spending, legacy spending, and charitable giving. Once a prospective retiree has estimated the cost of his or her core lifestyle needs, and calculated the income and withdrawals necessary, they will be able to see whether or not they'll have any excess capacity. Not surprisingly, taking into account the impact of compounding—and the reduction in compounding that occurs as a result of withdrawals—a retiree's spending rate is the key driver of all decisions. While marital status, gender, health-care costs, and tax status all influence the rate of spending, spending even 4 or 5 percent of assets annually is dangerous. Why? Because the headwinds of mediocre or even poor market returns, higher than anticipated inflation, taxes, and the blessing of longevity may quickly deplete savings for retirement.

Again, earlier retirement spending will have a greater impact on younger retirees because of the lost potential of compounding on the remaining assets, and such spending will also affect allocation decisions. Generally speaking, the allocations in a typical retirement portfolio allocation will skew toward bonds as a retiree ages. However, there is an important tradeoff between lowering volatility with more bonds, and building excess capacity with stocks, especially if core needs put assets at risk over time. As many have discovered in 2009, this can lead to a seriously crimped lifestyle.

Let's look at this in terms of my earlier discussion of the neuroscience of decision making. In much the same way that we can be victims of our own natural human fallibilities when confronted with certain problems of mathematics or probability, we must also recognize that our minds are hardwired for instant gratification. Research has shown us that when a child is told she can have one marshmallow now, or two marshmallows in five minutes, she may valiantly try to postpone her satisfaction, but she will almost always succumb and decide in favor of the one, immediate marshmallow. This, too, may be the result of natural selection—that is, if you don't eat today, you may not be around to eat tomorrow. (Interestingly enough, this study was followed-up years later, when the same children were in their teens, and those few who could restrain themselves as youngsters tended to have higher SAT scores. Of course, this may mean that IQ is inversely correlated with a taste for marshmallows.)

Children, of course, are not the only culprits. Americans only began saving again, after having passed through whole decades living on credit, when the current recession forced them to reevaluate their longer-term prospects. We needn't depend, however, on economic conditions to encourage saving. Imagining a number of different futures, for instance, each affected by the decisions we make today, is one powerful tool we can use to counter the "I want it and I want it now" mindset. Only when we can begin to think realistically about ourselves in the future—creating, one might say, memories of things to come—and not make the mistake of seeing our current selves 20 or 30 years from now, can we succeed at making time a key element of risk assessment.

In corporate management, a clear distinction exists between *line* jobs and *staff* jobs. The line managers actually operate the business, while the staff roles are advisory in nature and generally involve control or planning functions. In the early years of my career at Citibank, I was promoted into a major line position, with 400 people and 20 Vice Presidents reporting to me. Inevitably, upper management changed and I was given a staff job. Over time, I was assigned larger and increasingly more important staff jobs. Finally, despite rising to the level of the Chairman's staff, I had had enough. I kept thinking: "I'm a line guy, and so why do I keep getting these staff jobs?" One day, though, it finally dawned on me that I loved the work I was doing. Perhaps as a result, I did my job very well, and I was paid an awful lot of money. I spoke to a close colleague about my change of heart, and after thinking for a moment he said: "You know, you are a good line guy—but whether you know it or not, you're an *unbelievably great* staff guy."

At first I was stunned to hear this. How could I have thought of myself as a line manager throughout my career, only to find out that my talents were really better suited to staff work? Afterward, however, my colleague's assessment began to please me more and more. Why? It revealed that I had strengths not even I understood, and what's more, that I had been able to put them to use.

The point is that we often want to be, or feel ourselves to be, something we are not. Worse yet, sometimes we want things that are simply not obtainable. While it is true that one cannot hit a home run unless you step up to the plate and swing, as you take your swings it is important to leave open the possibility that you might, for instance, do better at pitching than hitting—or if at the plate, consider a slap-single to move the man on first to second. This is true in the world of investments too, where people who wish for outsize returns, rather than steady gains, often strike out. And one can only hope they do not do so if they do so in the bottom of the ninth, when there is no longer any time to recover.

Setting realistic time expectations is important in nearly every aspect of life. If we do not, we create unnecessary anxiety. I, for one, believe that meetings should be held in conference rooms without chairs. Thus, those attending would never have the opportunity to get comfortable, and would instead make their contributions quickly, saving everyone a lot of time. Unfortunately, my conference room has chairs—although I've gone to great pains to make sure they're not too comfortable. As well, for meetings that usually take 60 minutes, I book conference rooms for only half that time. Why? Because I believe in Parkinson's Principle, which holds that work expands to meet the time available. In other words, even if people are accustomed to certain jobs requiring a set amount of time, they will find a way to accomplish the same thing in less time if they must. That said, it takes nine months to have a baby, and some meetings really *do* require more time. Sometimes people *need* to stake out their positions, and then slowly come around to a single point of view. And if that's the case, and you budget 30 minutes for a meeting knowing full well it will probably last an hour, chances are the anxiety level will rise—unnecessarily—from the thirty-first minute on.

A Story of Risk: Part 11

In the late 1990s even someone who made their investment decisions by putting on a blindfold and throwing darts at a list of stocks would have made pretty good money, and that was a very good thing for Rob, because he'd used that approach for almost every decision he'd made in the last 20 years. Unfortunately, not all of those decisions had panned out as well as his stock picks during the tech boom. Had he invested his trust fund across a broad range of equities and fixed-income vehicles when he took control of it, he would have been a far wealthier man, but after a few years as a stock broker he began to make considerably more money than he had as a private banker, and so he finally gave up his rent-controlled apartment and moved into another, newer high-rise on the Upper East Side.

He and Lisa gradually fell out of touch with the friends who had introduced them, most of whom had begun to raise their own families. But the City was full of people, quite a few of whom seemed to show up in Rob's office. There they were all treated to his well-rehearsed speech about how the value of the stock market doubled every ten years—although he never pointed out exactly which ten years those were. It hardly mattered. The 1990s were the era of the new paradigm, and investors who wanted steady returns should buy a few T-bills and waste someone else's time. Didn't the words "opportunity of a lifetime," mean anything to you, he'd ask prospective investors. There was a tidal wave of opportunity rolling in toward the shore, and if you wanted to ride it, Rob was your man.

Rob's parents, unfortunately, were unable to ride that wave. They had dipped, and then scooped into their retirement savings to maintain their lifestyle, and had had to down-size twice since Rob graduated. Finally, they moved to Florida, where Rob's father began to have trouble remembering things. Given the downward arc of his last decade, this was a small blessing. His hearing was going too, and this was a *large* blessing, since his third wife had a very good memory, and was fond of referring to that downward arc in less than flattering terms.

Max had passed through the critical five-year post-operative period with no recurrence of his cancer, and had not only launched a promising career in banking, but had fulfilled that promise. He had started out in line jobs, with an ever greater number of bankers reporting to him, and then had side-stepped into risk management. The field was new when he entered it, just after the savings and loan crisis of the late 1980s and early 1990s, and as the field's importance grew, so did his stature in the banking world.

His own approach to investment had undergone a great change since the early days of stock picking on the NASDAQ, and despite having little cash on hand after the surgery that saved his life, his retirement funds and the boys' college accounts had remained intact. During the 1990s they had then soared, benefiting both from the lessons he'd learned at work and the diversified but dynamic approach to investing he'd adopted. His income, in the meantime, had skyrocketed as well, and while he and his wife lived well, they never came close to spending all the money he made. In fact, he had begun to spend almost as much time managing his charitable giving as he did managing his personal portfolio, with the bulk of that money directed toward cancer research. In short, Max was discovering that his risk aversion was growing as he grew older, and his goals changed.

Rob, meanwhile, after the birth of his daughter, had awakened one morning and had begun to curse his earlier, stubbornly cautious approach to investing. His assets had grown, of course, but they had barely kept pace with inflation, and given his lifestyle, he had never managed to add much to them. Now, however, he felt that the time had come, and throwing caution to the wind he moved his trust fund in its entirety into the one sector that epitomized the new paradigm—tech stocks. After all, it was never too late to make a killing in the markets.

PART | 4

REEVALUATION

Risk Principle | 12

MONITOR OUTCOMES CONTINUOUSLY

"Boundaries are to protect life, not to limit pleasures."
—Edwin Louis Cole

A close friend of mine is an oncologist, and over the past 30 years he has built up a thriving practice. I wish his specialty weren't necessary, but it is, and I like to think that his success is a measure of the good he has done in the world.

Recently, he and I passed a relaxing afternoon in his backyard. It was a beautiful fall day, and after eating a good meal, and putting away a bottle of fine wine, we began to discuss our work. For reasons I no longer remember I idly asked him the following question: What was the most startling thing he had observed over the course of his career? He didn't need time to think his answer over. In all the years he had practiced, he said, only *two* of the thousands of patients he had treated had attempted to change their lives after they were diagnosed with cancer. All of the others just wanted to continue doing what they had always done—that is, getting up in the morning, having breakfast, going to work, coming home for dinner with their families, and then falling asleep in an easy chair while watching TV.

Even in extraordinary circumstances, then, it seems that all most of us want to do is to maintain our present lifestyles. Even though we're aware that our lives constantly change, sometimes for better and sometimes for worse, we wish more than anything else to resist that change. It is one of the subtler ironies of life, therefore, that we need a sense of what the future may look like in order to do that.

Peter Drucker once said that the best way to predict the future is to *create* it. Scenario construction and analysis fits the bill perfectly, and without forcing us to wait to see what the future will bring. Constructing scenarios also involves the creation of boundaries, and de-risking our plans involves deciding how to remain within them. In essence, scenarios are "what if" stories that allow us to consider almost anything that can happen, both positive and negative, and help us to frame our responses. I stress the need for both negative and positive scenarios, because if you consider only the many things you might lose, or the possibility that your plans might fail—instead of the many things you might gain, and the possibility of success—you'll use only one part of this highly useful tool.

While I worked at Citibank, I slowly realized that banks were really just mirrors of the economic environment of the day. If the economy was doing well, and the bank's customers prospered, the bank generally did well. Conversely, when the economy was in trouble, and the bank's customers did poorly, it did not matter how well you understood credit—that is, risk asset acceptance criteria (RAAC) or existing loan performance—because the bank was unlikely to be asked to extend it, at least under terms favorable to our business. Nonetheless, when I was asked to develop the first enterprise risk management system for Citibank I knew I needed to understand not only the present economic environment, but the economic environments in which we would one day find ourselves. To do this we used scenarios.

Herman Kahn, who developed the concept while at the RAND Corporation in the 1950s, working for the U.S. military, is considered one of the fathers of scenario building. His early work dealt with the risks of nuclear war, and thus involved scenarios that would render most of our risk management useless. (Whenever I consider his work, I can't help but think back to the time we were asked if our bank vault would float in the event a tidal wave hit New York City—as if a bank vault, whether or not it would float down the Hudson River, would be of any interest to the survivors of such an event. Kahn was also one of the founders of the Hudson Institute, and when I launched the scenarios program at Citibank I had the privilege of working with one of his successors, Irv Levinson, the former Chief Researcher at the Hudson Institute.)

Scenarios, as I noted above, are really stories about the future. To construct them, one begins by listing the possible drivers of change, and then dividing them into two broad domains. The first is made up of those things we *believe* we know something about—generally trends that can be somewhat safely extrapolated from the past. We can, for example, safely make assumptions about long-term shifts in demographics. The second domain is made up of uncertainties such as interest rates, changes in political power, and as yet unforeseen innovations. Good scenario planning requires a careful blending of these two domains—the known and the unknown drivers of change—which result in a number of often inconsistent views of the future. A scenario regarding the start of World War III, for instance, might read as follows:

In 2015, after years of increasing hostilities along their borders, India and Pakistan went to war. Pakistan's ground forces proved to be superior at the outset of the conflict, but India's air force ruled the skies. International bodies were unable to bring the nations to the bargaining table, and as the war continued both countries enlisted the support of their allies.

Soon more than a dozen nations were involved. Pakistan depended on the support of its economic allies, most of whom had earned independence after the collapse of the USSR. With the notable exception of Georgia, these countries—Turkmenistan, Uzbekistan, Kyrgyzstan, Tajikistan, Azerbaijan, Kazakhstan, and Armenia—believed their economic interests to be aligned with Pakistan's military objectives, and thus contributed to its defense. India, instead, rallied the support of its friends in Bangladesh and Nepal, and attempted to enlist China as well, whose borders were put at risk by the conflict.

Approximately a year after the war began, China, sensing that they could no longer watch from afar, amassed troops along the Pakistani border. Pakistan, knowing that it would be unable to defend itself against the ground forces of both China and India, employed its nuclear arsenal, and World War III began.

You might just as reasonably concoct a scenario in which Pakistan and India joined forces against Islamic terrorism. Then, teasing out the least likely drivers of change, and comparing the two scenarios, you could whittle down the possibilities and consider the potential results. Scenarios like these have many advantages—the first of which, clearly, is that we do not need to fight World War III to consider its consequences. Even if they are not necessarily predictive, scenarios can challenge our present views of the world, long before events have changed them. And in so doing they provide us with "trip wires," and when we stumble across them, much like speed bumps make us aware of our speed, they lead us to reconsider where we are and what we're doing.

I have discussed the use of trip wires in earlier chapters, and they serve the same purpose within scenarios (as evidenced by their use in the White House Situation Room). Once the broad parameters of a scenario are in place, one begins to look for inflection points—or trip wires—that can be monitored to determine whether the events of the day might trigger a chain of events leading toward the fulfillment of the scenario. In other words, trip wires alert you to changes in circumstances that might affect the scenario. In the World War III scenario above, for example, I would put trip wires in place to monitor: (1) the relationship between Pakistan and India, (2) the relationship between China and Pakistan, and (3) the willingness of the UN to step in should border tensions flare up. If circumstances changed—for instance, if Russia warned that it would enter the fray should Chinese troops set foot on Pakistani soil—I would stop, write another scenario, and start paying attention to another set of trip wires.

When I worked at Citibank in the 1980s, one of our favorite trip wires was consumers' use of credit cards. The rise or fall in credit card debt is an inflection point—when debt increases history tells us that the economy is starting to improve, because consumer consumption is two-thirds of the U.S. economy. Therefore, if credit card use began to expand, we would react by slowly loosening credit controls, extending credit first to our most creditworthy customers, and then gradually begin to work with our second-tier customers. The point is that a large financial institution is like an oil tanker—when the ship is underway it's very difficult to turn quickly, and when it's stopped, a certain amount of time is necessary to get it back up to speed.

Another factor we monitored was the local movement of high net worth individuals' capital. Local capital flowing out of the country signaled the beginning of problems—best understood, after all, by those in the country—and foretold the eventual devaluation of that country's currency. If, instead, we had waited until local governments took action themselves, instead of monitoring capital flow ourselves, it would already have been too late to react.

Scenarios thus prevent us from being lulled into thinking that our own view of the world *is the only possible view*. This sort of mental trap, which we all risk falling into at one time or another, is related to our desire to maintain our personal lifestyles. We often judge our ability to do so by monitoring only local information, and ignoring information farther afield. And while it is most important for us to chart our own courses in life, and to make the decisions we believe to be in the best interests of our families, our friends, our businesses, and our communities, we often make these decisions based on insufficient information.

Without such information, gathered in a timely fashion, we tend to stay rigidly on course long after the tide has begun to shift against us. The viewpoints of dissidents, discussed in an earlier chapter, are one means of combating this tendency. Like Krugman's loss of faith in the Asian Tiger, the voices of dissidents can alert us to information we have missed, or ignored, and thus give us the time to make changes to our plans before events move out ahead of us.

You can write scenarios, track warning signs, and set up trip wires within an *industry* too, staying on the lookout for signs of change in the specific economy that most affects you. You can do the same to minimize the risk of losing your job, or if that can't be helped, to save and invest the money you need to secure your future while you have an income, taking into account that your contributions over time may not be constant. With the proper trip wires in place, you will know if the time has come to downsize your house, reduce your retirement contributions, or decrease your discretionary spending—*before* you have to. Once again, not doing anything often incurs the highest risk, and scenarios and trip wires allow you to move proactively before events begin to move you.

All of these techniques, it's easy to see, presume certain boundaries—drawn according to the needs of national security, corporate stability, or personal goals—and are designed to keep you within the lines you yourself have drawn. Your business scenarios, as a result, will most likely *not* include the possibility of a Chinese invasion of India, nor will your international scenarios include the possibility of an asteroid striking Earth. The point is that each set of trip wires, or each possible scenario, operates only within the boundaries you've set for yourself.

Perhaps a more commonplace example will help make the point. I recently took one of my younger sons bowling, and was surprised to see that bowling lanes no longer have mechanical bumpers that prevent you from throwing a gutter ball. (These bumpers were responsible for many of the points I scored as a child.) Those bumpers, just like the boundaries we create, not only increased the number of pins that went down, they kept me from bowling in someone else's lane—that is, straying outside the boundaries of the game. The point isn't that you should depend on the bumper every time you roll the ball, but that if you have boundaries in place, and you do shoot wide, they'll keep you from straying outside the game.

Sam Zell, the noted real estate investor, sold his huge real estate holdings at the top of the market. How? He had trip wires and scenarios in place that alerted him to the end of the real estate boom. When asked how he knew it was time to sell, he simply said: "You're either a buyer or a seller, and at some point I was no longer a buyer."

Of the many other tools that can be used to help you stay within your boundaries one of my personal favorites is a decision-weighting matrix. Very simply, it *quantifies* the factors decision makers deem most important, thus allowing them to evaluate the alternatives in a systematic way. Suppose, for example, I had to evaluate two potential job offers and was undecided as to which one to take. To begin, I would determine the general factors that are most important to me, and then rate each on a scale from 1 to 10 (with 10 being the most important). The initial matrix might look like the following:

Job Characteristics

Ability to advance	8
Fit with my personality	9
Money	8
Distance from home	7

This matrix makes it clear that the fit of the job is more important to me than how close the job is to my home. It is also more important than salary or the ability to advance. I could then evaluate alternative job offers in terms of the values assigned to the characteristics above. That subsequent matrix, if I were trying to decide between working for the U.S. government in Washington, D.C., or in private industry for the ABC Company, whose plant is not far from my home, would look something like this:

Job Characteristics	Government	ABC
Ability to advance (8)	6	7
Fit with personality (9)	7	8
Money (8)	8	9
Distance from home (7)	4	9

Finally, I would weigh the alternatives by multiplying the values of the first matrix with those of the second, giving me a finished grid like the following:

Job Characteristics	Government	ABC
Ability to advance	48	56
Fit with personality	63	72
Money	64	72
Distance from home	28	63
	203	263

While it is clear in this example that the better choice for me is the ABC job, I have seen matrix calculations of this sort come down to a single point difference between the alternatives. In a sense, just like an experienced accountant's ability to see that the numbers on a spread sheet are clearly outside normal

parameters, and most likely the result of a mistaken calculation, you will most likely understand the results of a decision-
weighting matrix long before you add up the final numbers. The
process itself, almost subconsciously, helps keep you within your
boundaries.

Monitoring

Whether your decisions are reached as a result of scenario planning, attention to trip wires, or decision-weighting matrixes, those
decisions do not *end* the process, they simply bring you to the next
stage—monitoring the results of those decisions.

Throughout my career, I must have read thousands of strategic
plans submitted to senior management. In those 35 years, I came
across only *one* that started with the projections from the *previous*
five-year plan, and then compared the actual results, five years later,
to that plan. Perhaps it's just human nature. Maybe we're hardwired
to look forward, not backward. But both businesses and individuals
seem to be far more skilled—and interested in—planning than they
are monitoring results. Skilled investors, on the other hand, insist
on one-year, three-year, and five-year track records for all portfolio
managers. It's one thing to consider various plans of attack, do your
research, and come to the wrong conclusion, but another entirely
not to monitor results and recognize your errors. What, after all, are
political elections, but referendums on past events—that is, the next
in an endlessly recurring round of decisions made by voters *after*
they have monitored the candidates'—or the political parties'—
results. Seen in this light, perhaps the most effective political slo-
gan of the last three or four decades, used by Clinton during his

campaign against George H. W. Bush, was: Are you better off today than you were four years ago?

Neither does monitoring necessarily occur only after decisions have been made. Think of your annual physical exam. One of its benefits depends on comparing this year's EKG with the results of a base EKG taken years earlier. In this case, the trip wire is the base reading, and if it moves higher you'll stumble. But the annual exam also has a value of its own, regardless of personal history, family history, or past illnesses. And its usefulness is based on process—first, collecting physical data; second, checking to see if those numbers fall within generally accepted boundaries; and third, constructing scenarios for the future. Does your complete blood count (CBC) indicate liver problems? Is your cholesterol outside normal boundaries? And if so, what is likely to happen if your count continues to rise without treatment, or without a change in lifestyle and diet? The annual physical exam is relatively inexpensive—certainly compared to a stay in the hospital—and involves monitoring a relatively simple set of data, and yet the exam is unquestionably preventative medicine's most effective tool.

A Story of Risk: Part 12

Rob celebrated his forty-eighth birthday at Tavern on the Green. He, just like New York City and the stock markets, had had a bad couple of years, but as long as he still had a credit card that wasn't maxed out he wasn't going to scrimp on his birthday. His wife felt the same way—and perhaps even more so when her birthday rolled around. In fact, they always tried to outdo each other's birthday gifts, expecting more themselves in return, and this year was no exception. Long before the party began, Lisa had asked one of Rob's closest friends at work to pick up the brand new Harley Davidson Roadster she'd bought her husband, and to drive it from the dealer's to the parking lot at Tavern on the Green. Once everyone arrived, she walked Rob outside, blindfolded, and then showed him his gift. He was like a boy on Christmas, and couldn't wait to start it up, especially since his friends had pitched in to buy them both helmets. Lisa wouldn't go near hers. She'd just had her hair done, and so Rob roared out of the parking lot on his own. What he didn't know was that she had used the same credit card to buy the motorcycle that he had planned on using to pay for the festivities. Later that evening, that discovery would make it a true surprise party.

Rob's birthday party, and its aftermath, were a microcosm of the life he and Lisa had lived for the past ten years, fueled by the dotcom boom. As the value of their stock portfolio soared, so did their cost of living. And when the crash finally came, they found themselves with very little in the bank, an income cut in half, and monthly bills they could no longer afford to pay.

Max and Barbara were hit hard by the crash too, but they stayed the course, letting their well-diversified portfolio ride out the storm. Max's brush with death, years earlier, had taught him to enjoy every day, but to prepare for the worst, and he had done so. He didn't make as much money in the markets as Rob did during the late 1990s, but on the other hand, he didn't lose nearly as much when the markets crashed. The markets' movements, in fact, meant very little to him. He was making very good money doing something he liked. His wife and his children were healthy, and while he didn't dwell on his past illness, he still saw his oncologist once a year, and when things went badly at work or at home he never failed to remind himself that there had been plenty of people in the waiting room that day that would be glad to have his troubles.

In fact, whenever he happened to discuss that terrible year with his close friends, he was fond of saying that it was one of the best things that had ever happened to him. Some of them misunderstood, believing he was talking about the lucky break that started his new career. But when they did, he'd just shake his head and say, no, that's not what I meant. The experience had taught him to see the difference between what he could control and what he couldn't, and he had promised himself he'd never again be caught unprepared. As the years went by, then, and he began to make more and more money, he and Barbara moved out of the city, but bought a house they could afford to live in even if he never worked again.

Driving toward home one night, Max turned on the radio and happened to come across an interview with a world famous blues musician. The interviewer, after having dispensed with the usual praise, asked the musician how he had managed to spend his entire professional life playing the 12-bar blues. Didn't he feel restricted, always stuck in the same old chord progressions? Didn't the format limit his powers of expression?

The musician, as politely as possible, told the interviewer he just didn't get it. Far from limiting his ability to express himself, the 12-bar blues created the boundaries within which he found musical freedom. Only within them, in fact, did he feel truly free to express himself.

Risk Principle | 13

IDENTIFY AND LEARN FROM YOUR MISTAKES

"A life spent making mistakes in not only more honorable, but more useful than a life spent doing nothing."
—George Bernard Shaw

The story of Ramchandran "Jai" Jaikumar is well-known to those in the manufacturing sciences, due to his seminal work on operations while a member of the Technology and Operations Management group at the Harvard Business School. That research, however, was but one small part of his life.

Born in Madras, India, and educated in the United States, Jaikumar was something of a modern-day peripatetic, and like Aristotle enjoyed discussing his ideas with his associates while walking or hiking in distant parts of the world. From his youth he was also an avid mountain climber, and made several "first ascents" of peaks around the world.

In December, 1966, when he was 22 years old, he and one of his most trusted friends reached the pinnacle of a 24,000-foot-high mountain in the Himalayas. They had begun the climb long before first light that morning, and although they had fixed 1:00 pm as their "turnaround time," they were so close to the peak by early afternoon they decided to push ahead rather than descend and prepare for another assault the next day. For one of them, it was a fatal error.

During their descent, as the daylight began to desert them, they made their way across a treacherous ice cornice, and worried about its ability to hold them, decided to untie the ropes that bound them together. That way, if one of them fell, the other would not be pulled after him. Moments later the cornice gave way beneath them, each of them falling in different directions. By the time Jaikumar finally came to rest, his climbing suit in shreds, his body battered, his equipment scattered, and his companion nowhere to be seen, he was 3,000 feet below the point at which he had fallen, and on the opposite face of the mountain from their base camp.

He walked for the next 20 hours, never sitting down, afraid that he might not be able to rise again. He felt certain he would never see his friend again, and wondered if he, too, would simply fall to the ground, and disappear under the next snow, never to be found. Nearly at the end of his strength, he came upon a small shepherd's hut, but collapsed before he could enter it. Hearing him fall, perhaps, a native woman came out, and over the next few hours she cleaned his wounds and gave him food and water. Neither could communicate with the other, although he used hand signals to indicate that he needed to get down the mountain.

The next day, although she was older than he was, and much smaller, she began to carry him down the mountain on her back. Every so often she'd stop to rest, and then hoist him up again. After three days, they arrived at her village, and there she arranged for his passage to the nearest hospital. Once the villagers put him on top of a donkey, and she saw that he was on his way, she started back up the hill. He never learned her name.

Despite his serious injuries, he quickly recovered. His friend's body was never found. Months later he returned to the village to attempt to repay his debt. Realizing that money had no meaning in the villagers' subsistence economy, he hit upon the idea of building a school. During the decades that followed, after emigrating to the United States, earning his PhD, beginning to teach, and starting his own company, he expanded his school-building efforts to far-off communities around the world. At the age of 54, he died of a heart attack while climbing in Ecuador. In his own words: "While my passion for climbing led me to scale that one particular peak, my fall helped me reach much greater heights . . ."

It's often been said about me that I make many mistakes, but that I never make the same mistake twice. I'd like to think that's true, but it's just as important to me that I be remembered for learning from those mistakes. Mistakes, after all, don't threaten the success of our goals—that is, not if they're identified and corrected—instead, they offer us the opportunity to fine tune the process through which we try to realize our goals. Identified and corrected mistakes also free us from their emotional costs, and just as importantly save us the time we have to spend dealing with them—often, ad infinitum. Seen in this light, the *discovery* of a mistake, whether it occurs in the beginning, the middle, or at the end of your investment time frame, can actually be considered a small victory.

The Japanese philosophy of Kaizen, or continual improvement, is based on just this approach—of making small, incremental changes that lead to the fulfillment of one's goals. First, opportunities for improvement are identified, and then small suggestions for improvement are tested in discrete locations. If the results are positive, the new techniques are adopted across the entire enterprise—and then the process of improvement begins again.

For the purposes of this book, I'd like to review mistakes made in two general categories: those made by individuals, or should we say made by individual investment advisors on behalf of their clients, and those made by institutions—that is, banks, investment management firms, financial rating firms, or government agencies. Some of these mistakes overlap, of course, while others fall into only one of the two categories.

Let's begin with errors made by individuals. First, each of us has a unique starting point, particular goals, and an individual plan formulated to reach those goals. Common mistakes occur within each of those spheres, and have varying impacts on results. Therefore, I'll review some of the common mistakes made in planning, in execution, in monitoring, and perhaps most importantly, mistakes made while rebalancing your portfolio—that is, mistakes made in reallocating your assets as your goals, your circumstances, and market conditions change around you.

Before doing that, however, investors must confront one irrefutable fact—as you attempt to realize the benefits from compounded investments there is no quantifiable difference between spending your portfolio, losing money in the markets, paying others to manage your money, paying your taxes, and losing buying power to inflation. All are costs, all have an identical effect on the earnings of your portfolio, and *all can be managed.* In the same way there is no difference, in terms of compounding, between contributing money to your portfolio and making money in the markets. Your contributions will change constantly, and sometimes may not even occur, just as your earnings will change constantly, and sometimes may even be reversed. If you fail to view all of your investment decisions from this perspective, then your plans and management controls will be compromised.

Again, I do not intend to trace the mistakes of individual investors over the past few years. But having seen a great many mistakes made over the years, I *can* categorize them using the principles I've laid out in this book. I won't attempt to compile an exhaustive list— because that list could fill another book—but will just point to some of the more common mistakes I've seen investors make.

Finally, individual investors, no matter their income level or wealth, have two essential choices: They can either manage their investments themselves, or pay others to do it for them. Whichever approach you adopt, identifying mistakes made within each of these essential tasks listed above can, and should, be viewed in light of the principles I've laid out in the earlier sections of this book, and to which I'll now turn.

No matter who manages your investments, all plans begin with *assessment*—in other words, you have to begin, as I did in this book, by asking yourself one simple question: Where am I now? In other words, what do I own, what do I owe, what do I earn, and what do I spend? As simple as these questions seem to be, individual investors frequently make mistakes as they answer them. Do you own your vacation home, for instance, or does the bank own it? In other words, what is your equity, or to what extent did you leverage your purchase? High net worth individuals tend not to have mortgages—unless the cost of borrowing falls below historic levels of return—and also tend to have assets that exceed the value of their homes. For them this question is both more easily answered, and less relevant. For those attempting to amass wealth, however, their house is usually their primary investment. They have to know, therefore, just how much of it is theirs. And overvaluing your assets, as I pointed out in Risk Principle 3, is a common, all too human error. This error compromises any investment plan, whether you design it, or someone else designs it for you.

This brings us to liquidity. If real estate accounts for a large percentage of your portfolio, then no matter the return, your holdings are relatively illiquid—especially during market downturns like those we've just experienced. Therefore, without a certain amount of liquid assets to help you through financial crises—or the loss of your primary source of income—you may have no choice but to sell your primary assets at the precise moment the market for them falls. The same is true of tax-deferred assets. While your 401(k) and 529 college plans are not subject to taxes, neither are they liquid—at least in terms of their nominal value. In other words, you could probably get more money—in terms of its historic market value—for your house as the real estate market was crashing and burning than you'd get after paying the onerous penalties for early withdrawals from tax-deferred accounts. Yes, the money is there, but no, you can't get to it in a crisis—that is, without destroying the benefits of compounding.

Finally, investors frequently make mistakes when estimating their earning and spending—and usually make them in opposite directions—and that sort of miscalculation during the planning stage can quickly undermine anyone's plans. This mistake afflicts both individuals trying to amass wealth, and high net worth individuals. And whether you invest yourself, or pay someone else to do it, mistakes made when calculating those numbers will compromise your goals.

Individual investors also frequently mistake the limits of their knowledge, no matter how much money they have in the bank. Oftentimes, they don't know exactly how their money is invested, exactly how their assets are allocated, or even who is actually managing their money. Failing to know what you don't know is a common and often disastrous mistake. And the simplest defense is to invest in financial instruments you understand, managed by people you know. Buying investments with high ratings, as we've seen over the past few years, or even working with money managers with good reputations, won't necessarily protect your portfolio if you don't have a fundamental understanding of the investment vehicles involved.

Individual investors also make frequent and serious mistakes regarding the *rules of the game*. These include failing to accurately determine your risk appetite *before* making investment decisions, and failing to demand transparency from those with whom you do business. Those who turn the management of their assets over to others frequently make this error—and often pay for it. Individual investors also make the mistake of concentration risk—that is, they fail to diversify their assets—and fail to establish the sort of checks and balances that will protect them from mistakes made by others. Finally, investors frequently forget that their plans must change as their goals change, and as the economy changes around them. To stick to your original plans as taxes, inflation, or your income rise and fall is a critical error. And this is true whether you manage your money, or someone else does.

While following all the principles of risk management will take you down the shortest and least dangerous path to your goals, failing to follow the principles of decision making may not only steer you off that path, but might actually send you off the cliff. Your decisions, on the other hand, are dependent on everything that comes before them, and so mistakes made during assessment, or in following the rules of the game, may well lead to decisions that jeopardize your goals. And this is true, once again, no matter who manages your investments.

Once it's time to make your decisions, one of the most frequent mistakes investors make is failing to consider all the alternatives. This, as I've pointed out before, is an error of omission, and errors of omission can be exceptionally costly. To begin with, considering all the options vastly increases your chances of success. And if you make a mistake, and treat it as an opportunity for learning, the mistake may actually prove to be a benefit over the long haul. If, however, you neglect to consider all the alternatives, a mistake will teach you very little—and force you to start all over again.

Ignoring the importance of exit strategies is another common investing mistake, and once made may make it extremely difficult for you to change course. This is especially true if you invest in vehicles that limit, or involve fees, for redemptions.

Those who haven't considered all the alternatives, and have left themselves without exit strategies, have usually made the mistake of failing to involve everyone in risk management. Avoiding this mistake means involving not only your advisor—if you don't manage your own assets—but your immediate family, your accountant, your lawyer, and anyone else you know who may be able to assist you. This, of course, implies a further responsibility—carefully checking the reputation of those you choose to help you reach your goals. Warren Buffett's take on that topic may well be the most quoted observation of the financial crisis: "It's only when the tide goes out that you find out who's been swimming naked."

Finally, individuals whose plans do not succeed often make the mistake of trying to "time" the market. Again, even a cursory review of the returns yielded by equities and fixed-income investments over the last 50 years—both domestic and foreign—demonstrate the importance of setting time frames for your investment decisions, and then sticking to them. And yet an astonishing number of investors continue to flee the market only after prices decline, then jump back in long after a rebound is underway, and in the process defeat the purpose of making their investment decisions within specific time frames, tailored to their goals. And these sorts of timing errors are mistakes whether they are made by those who handle their own investments, or whether they are forced upon those who make your decisions for you.

Monitoring the results of your decisions—or reevaluation—is the final step in the risk management process, and yet failing to continually review the outcomes of your decisions is one of the most common mistakes investors make. Making honest assessments, learning the rules of the game, and making sound decisions are all intended to produce *general* results tailored to your goals, but any number of mistakes made along the way—to say nothing of unforeseeable changes in the markets, or the economy itself—may force you to reconsider your strategies. Avoiding this final step, therefore—and it should have a fixed place on your quarterly calendar—may put all your previous efforts at risk.

Having created a short list of some of the most common mistakes made by individual investors, let's turn now to mistakes made by institutions. While I'm not suggesting that individuals should attempt to influence the decisions made by large financial institutions, a familiarity with their inner workings is valuable on a number of levels—especially when deciding where to put your trust.

As I pointed out in an earlier chapter, one of the most colossal errors I witnessed during my 30-year career was the demise of the risk culture at Citibank. And despite my personal certainty that every person in a company has to be a risk manager, those words carry little weight in large organizations unless they are echoed by the CEO. In other words, upper-level management sets the example—or doesn't—and company personnel react accordingly. Therefore, as I wrote earlier, when I learned that Citigroup's executives had discarded the Windows on Risk program, I sold my stock in the company.

Of course there were other signs, too. When I worked at Citibank, promotions to senior jobs were contingent on credit signing authority. And you didn't get credit signing authority unless you had demonstrated a thorough knowledge of the fundamentals of credit, and had had years of experience putting them into practice. That body of knowledge included, but was not limited to, a comprehensive understanding of Risk Asset Acceptance Criteria (RAAC), the proven ability to monitor portfolio exposure, a fundamental understanding of recovery procedures, the ability to offer strategic support for the bank's products and services, and expertise in credit approval and product and business development. If you failed once, you were put on a watch list. If you failed twice, you lost your credit signing authority—you were defrocked, in other words, like a priest who failed to uphold his vows. Shortly after I left Citibank, however, it was easy to see that new management not only had no experience running a bank, but had no credit orientation—and knowing when to extend credit, and when to deny it, is the foundation on which successful banks are built.

The sort of mistakes that caused Citibank's recent troubles were not limited to the banking sphere. General Motors, and to a lesser extent Ford and Chrysler, have provided us with textbook examples over the past 40 years.

After the first oil embargo in 1973—brought on both by the Arab invasion of Israel and oil exporters' wishes to control the price of their most precious commodity—American car manufacturers undertook a short-lived campaign to reduce the wheel base and gross weight of their cars in order to improve fuel economy. These innovations, partly a response to higher gasoline prices and corresponding shifts in the tastes of the car-buying public, were also the result of Corporate Average Fuel Economy (CAFE) standards mandated by Congress in 1975. Those standards, however, imposed higher mile per gallon requirements for passenger cars, and lower requirements for light trucks (the weight base for which was raised over time, thus protecting a whole range of "crossover" vehicles like minivans and SUVs from fuel efficiency standards). Oil prices declined in the late 1970s, but the oil price shock that accompanied the war between Iran and Iraq, in 1982, made the gasoline-buying public almost nostalgic for the good old days of 1973.

Given my earlier discussion of scenario construction, the history of automobile design in America over the last three decades seems almost absurd, if not actually insane. After 1973, little imagination was necessary to create scenarios for future oil shocks, as a result either of geopolitical events—for instance, the invasion of Israel, the war between Iraq and Iran, and the Gulf Wars—or changes in the economic environment—like China's rising economic power, and the corresponding increase in its demand for petroleum, or the easy credit after the dotcom bust and 9/11 that led to speculation in real estate and commodities.

Nonetheless, GM prepared for all but the inevitable rise in oil prices by producing ever larger SUVs and trucks, a plan which culminated in the introduction of the Hummer, a consumer version of the military vehicle used in the Gulf Wars. Neither were consumers blameless. Foreign car manufacturers, long accustomed to higher oil prices, offered a variety of fuel-efficient automobiles, but Americans continued to snap up Sport Utility Vehicles, seen bouncing along mountain roads in television commercials, but in reality most often parked in the lots of shopping malls or in front of elementary schools.

While examples of individual and corporate mistakes abound, examples of learning from those mistakes are more difficult to identify. The Tylenol poisoning scare of the early 1980s, however, provides a shining example. When seven persons died after taking potassium cyanide–laced capsules, and Tylenol's market share plummeted, parent company Johnson & Johnson reacted quickly. To begin, it recalled tens of millions of bottles of the pain relief medicine from around the nation, even though the deaths all occurred in the vicinity of Chicago. And while manufacturing standards were not to blame, the company quickly realized that it had failed to anticipate the possibility of sabotage and took aggressive measures to ensure product safety. When the capsules were reintroduced two months later, the packaging featured a series of safeguards making them essentially tamper-proof. And while those of us with weak grips or short fingernails have been struggling to get to our medicine ever since, Johnson & Johnson's response created an industry standard for package protection still in force today.

To end, I'd like to turn to a short review of the institutional errors behind the recent financial crisis—in a sense, applying the principles I've discussed in the body of this book to the events discussed at its beginning.

Perhaps the most enduring lesson of the credit crisis associated with the recent financial crisis is the central role played by liquidity. The Basel Committee on Banking Supervision made the following distinction between types of liquidity:

> *Funding liquidity risk* is the risk that the firm will not be able to meet efficiently both expected and unexpected current and future cash flow and collateral needs without affecting either daily operations or the financial conditions of the firm. *Market liquidity risk* is the risk that a firm cannot easily offset or eliminate a position at the market price because of inadequate market depth or market disruption.[*]

During the financial crisis, liquidity dried up for large segments of the fixed-income and commercial paper markets, leading to financial gridlock, and thus the inability to set observable prices. This gridlock caused a complex, interconnected system to come close to failure. While many investors still see this as the result of financial recklessness on the part of the nation's largest investment

---

[*] Basel Committee on Banking Supervision, 2008.

banks, the primary institutional error lay in failing to understand the degree to which the loss of liquidity would affect the normal activities of the entire financial system.

Liquidity, naturally enough, can be thought of in terms of water, and to understand the consequences of the loss of liquidity one need only think of ice. Yes, it's water, but it no longer flows. During the crisis, when the markets for certain financial instruments froze, so did the ability of financial institutions to sell other assets to raise cash to cover their liabilities, thus leading to the sort of *financial liquidity risk* defined above.

An over-reliance on the Efficient Market Hypothesis also proved to be a critical mistake. In normal markets, prices are observable, and even less sophisticated investors can enter or leave the market according to their needs for diversification. When markets freeze, however, prices often have to plummet far below their *intrinsic* value before buyers will reenter the market.

Another critical mistake involved counterparty exposure. When Lehman Brothers collapsed, not only were losses spread throughout the system, but the collateral upon which many financial arrangements depended disappeared. This led to the forced sale of less liquid assets—think of the example I used in Risk Principle 4 regarding the effects of a large investor's redemptions from a hedge fund—which further weakened the financial health of institutions indirectly harmed by Lehman Brother's failure.

The growth in securitized assets, the value of which was dependent on sophisticated analytical and statistical modeling, constituted another fundamental error. Taking MBS as an example, the complex instruments that allowed investors access to new asset classes did not offer the sort of "drive-by" valuation that might have revealed fundamental errors in cash flow projections, given the viability of the subprime mortgages on which they depended.

As I wrote above, it is not my intention to undertake a systematic review of the causes of the financial crisis, or to use these pages to propose a comprehensive solution to the behavior that led to it. Nonetheless, given the examples above, the following proposals, made in light of the risk management principles introduced in this book, might help prevent the recurrence of many of the problems that led to the recent crisis.

- Empower senior line mangers with risk management responsibility and autonomy.
- Provide clear product definitions and investment boundaries to satisfy client expectations and stated risk appetites.
- Maintain a strong, centralized new product approval process.
- Create understandable policies and procedures and ensure they are followed.
- Design operations so that they are driven by client needs and expectations. This entails clarifying ambiguous investment guidelines and learning from errors to ensure they do not recur any place in the organization.
- Promote extensive communication and dialogue about risk taking and risk management at all levels.
- Sustain a governance process composed of various firm-wide and business-unit-specific risk committees.
- Implement an industrial strength compliance function.
- Integrate the risk functions with compliance and an internal audit.

To sum, it is critically important for both individuals and institutions to recognize errors when they occur, to correct them quickly, and to put processes into place to ensure they will not be repeated. To do this we need to know exactly *what* went wrong, and *how* it affected operations, results, or relationships. This is especially true because mistakes aren't discrete events, disconnected from everything around them. They are more like communicable diseases, and once they infect a single environment can easily spread from place to place, or from person to person—as anyone who has opened an email attachment without anti-virus software can attest.

Or, of course, you can adopt an even simpler, perfectly effective approach, and never make a single mistake: Simply do nothing.

A Story of Risk: Part 13

When he turned 50, and looked back over his youth, it seemed to Max as if he had made one mistake after another, with one great exception—marrying his wife, and having children. He had mistaken gambling on penny stocks for investing as a young man, losing far more than he gained. He had failed to consider the possibility that he might *need* to change jobs, or might *want* to change professions, and that if he did, his income might disappear for months. And having failed to foresee this possibility, and to prepare for it by establishing reasonable cash reserves, when he did find himself out of work he was forced to take a job that not only wouldn't pay the bills, but cut into the time he needed to search for another job. He had also failed to understand that the money he had put aside for his kids' college tuition and his retirement was all but locked away, and given the penalties involved with early withdrawals, would not help him through short-term financial difficulties. Finally, when he became sick, he realized that he had made the mistake of confusing happiness with wealth. Lying there in the hospital he had not been afraid of losing his life savings, but of losing his family.

Having made those mistakes, however, he had learned from them. And while he could not absolutely prevent another serious illness, he had quit smoking, had adopted a healthier diet, and had made the gym part of his daily routine. Now, at mid-life, in possession of nearly every material comfort he could want, and well-protected from the financial uncertainties of life, it was easier than ever for him to place his material success in perspective. His money made him wealthy, but his family made him rich.

Rob was neither wealthy, nor rich. Nor had he learned much from his mistakes. When he first took control of his trust fund, he was extraordinarily risk averse, and given his family history invested only in bonds. His strategy succeeded perfectly. He not only kept his money, he even made a little. Unfortunately, the costs of goods and services were soaring, and so his money didn't buy what it used to. Then, when he lost his job at the bank and started to work as a stock broker, he not only decided to dump all his money into equities, but to dump it all into just one sector—technology. In fact, he didn't even believe he was *risking* his capital, given the new paradigm. The old rules were for investment dinosaurs.

At least he was getting a lot of use out of his birthday motorcycle, because when Lisa divorced him she kept the BMW—and custody of their daughter. Rob tried not to let it bother him, that is, no more than having lost his job as a stock broker bothered him. He was better off on his own, he told himself, and that's pretty much what he was—on his own—after losing his wife, his daughter, and his job. At least he still had some money—that is, the same five hundred grand he'd coddled for years. Only a year or two earlier he had owned several million dollars in tech stocks, but when the dotcom bubble burst, the value of his portfolio fell to just over a million—and more than half of that went to his ex-wife and his lawyer.

In short, he was done in New York. He had no family, no job, and few real friends, and so he decided to take a cross-country trip on his bike. He had a friend out in Vegas, someone he used to work with when he was a banker, and the guy told him there were fortunes to be made in real estate out in Vegas. Especially for anyone who had a little seed money.

CONCLUSION

Risk Principle | 14

ENDURING PRINCIPLES AND PERPETUAL PROCESS

"The inevitable takes a long time to happen,
but when it does, it happens quickly."
—David Martin

We often speak of the courage necessary to face death, but the truth is that everyone faces death from the moment they're born. Death is inevitable. Most of us, however, think of it in such remote terms that we don't really face it at all. As a result, when the end finally appears, few of us are prepared. It is at that moment, when death is *imminent,* and there is no possibility of escape, that courage comes into the picture.

The alternative—not to death, but to facing it before we are ready—is thoughtful, timely preparation; or in other words, to make decisions before we are *forced* to make them; before certain inevitabilities, so long on the horizon, appear unexpectedly in front of us, and we no longer have the time to consider the alternatives; when we can still calmly and intelligently assess our circumstances, consider our alternatives, and make informed decisions, monitoring the results as we go. This is what I refer to as "de-risking," and although the principles set out here are drawn from my experience as a risk manager at a number of leading investment firms, they apply not only to financial matters, but to almost every decision you'll make over the course of your life.

Successfully de-risking your investments, to say nothing of your life plans, means that when lightning strikes, as it almost certainly will at one time or another, your plans, and the processes you have put in place to accomplish them, will make courage unnecessary—or in other words, will protect you from jeopardizing your goals by having to make decisions in the heat of the moment, without having first considered the risks. Those who do not are usually caught without a chair when the music stops; those who do are *already* sitting down.

Put another way, wise men and women understand that certain risks are necessary in order to achieve their goals—but they determine their appetite for risk, and make their decisions regarding it, *before* the storm arrives—because every decision itself incurs a risk. In fact, even doing nothing incurs a risk. And this is as true in our personal lives as it is in the world of finance.

Not long ago I spoke to a neuroscientist at Cambridge University about the impact of video games on the risk-taking appetite of the next generation. He believed that because success in these games depends on early pattern recognition, the games taught young persons to take *inordinate* risks in order to discover such patterns, and what's more, that their expanded appetite for risk might extend to their behavior in the real world too, putting them in harm's way. Afterward I wished I had asked him whether he had any children born in the 1990s. If he had, he would have been able to observe the natural human growth of his children alongside the growth of video gaming. Risk taking, in fact, is a critical part of most video games, and the games reward those who are willing to chance "death" over and over again—an integral part of the games' learning processes. The gamers do so, however, with the knowledge that a push of the button is all they need to be "reborn." Whether or not these experiences will help create a generation with too great an appetite for risk is uncertain, but one thing is sure—just like Star Wars put an end to boys playing cowboys and Indians, changes in technology will lead to changes in risk taking. One need only look to the growth of computer-aided "micro-trading," which makes day-trading look like long-term investing by comparison, to see that this is true.

There will always be new financial instruments, new markets, and new risks, but sound principles of risk management and the frameworks for decision making will remain pretty much the same. I, for instance, learned the mathematics of hedging from a professor at MIT who ran a seminar at Citibank. In those days, the Hewlett-Packard 12C was the Cadillac of calculators for finance professionals. Every time our mentor pointed out another wrinkle in a complex hedging strategy he would give us practice examples—or scenarios—so that we could see the principle in action. His first words always were: "Take a deep breath, take out your 12C, and turn it on." The point is, that even if a concept appears at first to be bewilderingly complex, it can almost always be understood by first dividing it into small, easily mastered tasks. Then, with patience and persistence you can comprehend and deal with almost any issue.

Mathematical models, though, as I've said before, are all but useless without human judgment. When I look to hire new risk managers, therefore, I always ask candidates what kind of hobbies they have. Good risk guys tend to be inquisitive, and as a result often choose, and master, highly unusual hobbies with very complex characteristics. Someone who sees such work as drudgery—like entering figures in a ledger—will never excel at it; those who do succeed tend to treat the work as if it were a game, like chess or bridge.

When faced with a difficult problem, I personally like to "roll in it" first, or as some people put it, "chew on it a long time before swallowing." The point is that you need to mentally circle the problem in order to understand all its ramifications before you can begin to deal with it effectively. Once you reach that point, all you need is a framework for making decisions, and a strong work ethic to see you through. You won't get it right every time, but you'll be right more often than you'll be wrong, and as the years pass the process will become almost automatic.

Occasionally you'll come up against new problems, ones for which experience has not prepared you, but a process will still provide you with a means for approaching them. Without such a process, we have to depend on courage, and courage is not something we can inherit, or which we can be taught, nor a thing we can always depend upon. Only when the moment comes will we know if we possess it. Continual preparation, however, in the light of fundamental, timeless principles, as well as the belief in your power to control certain events, *can* be encouraged, and that is why I wrote this book.

Risk, like the inevitability of death, is always present. Only when the outcomes of your decisions are imminent, however, will you know whether you managed your risks well, or will need to rely on courage.

A Story of Risk: Part 14

The longer he lived in Las Vegas, the more Rob wondered why he hadn't headed west earlier. The East Coast now seemed as remote as Europe had when he lived in New York, and its customs and landscape just as foreign. It was his father's and grandfather's world, not his, and even though it had taken him his whole adult life to realize it, he had never really belonged there. Vegas was his kind of town, thrown up overnight in the thin air of the high desert, without history, culture, or social convention. Its neon-lit streets, buzzing with electricity every single night, existed for one reason— to draw those looking for easy money to the casinos, like moths to a flame, and to send them home with their wallets empty.

In that sense it wasn't altogether different from banking or the stock market—at least the way Rob saw it—but those were old games, with too many rules, and they took too long to play. Things happened fast out in the desert, and the strip wasn't the only place you could make money. The way Rob and his new business partner, Donnie, saw it, the casinos were just like savings and loans. Gamblers made their deposits every night, and that capital fueled growth around the strip. And that's where Rob and Donnie came in.

Donnie ran the construction end of the business, and Rob handled sales, and together they were building and selling houses almost as fast as Ford made pickup trucks. New York was a vertical city, and the only place to build was up. But the Southwest, as flat as a parking lot, was just one big subdivision stretching out toward the horizon. And five years into the new century business was booming, and houses were popping up like flowers in the desert after a rain.

As Rob's sales staff began to sell more houses than Donnie could build, Rob asked himself why he shouldn't try to combine what he'd learned in the world of banking with the opportunity he'd stumbled upon in the great Southwest. Why just stick to sales, which were limited by the number of houses they could build? Why not start a mortgage business, and get in on everyone's action? Donnie and Rob had a thriving construction business, but house builders were swarming around Las Vegas like bees in an apple orchard, and every house they built needed a mortgage.

Donnie thought it was the best idea he'd heard of since someone started selling beer at gas stations, and within a month the Golden Sunset Mortgage Co., Inc. had moved into office space in a strip mall in Henderson. Rob made calls to some of his old friends in New York, and in the meantime put a collection of car salespeople, government retirees, and army veterans to work. Before long they were turning out mortgages faster than the U.S. Treasury could print money.

No one was turned away. Those with bad credit, and those whose income couldn't be verified, paid higher rates, and everyone else picked and chose from mortgage options as varied as flavors in an ice cream emporium. Golden Sunset offered fixed mortgages, adjustable rate mortgages, interest only mortgages, and for a select group of five or ten thousand, mortgages that required no down payments. Those mortgages never gathered dust on the desks of the originators. A day or two after the closing ceremonies, they were resold to banks, and eventually found their way to either Fannie Mae or Freddie Mac. Before three months had gone by, Golden Sunset had all but taken over the strip mall, squeezing a nail salon and a dog groomer out of their monthly leases. By the time six months had passed, they began to see repeat business, as those who had seen the value of their houses skyrocket began to flip their three-bedroom houses for four bedrooms and a pool.

A year after Rob arrived in Las Vegas, Max and Barbara sat on folding chairs in Harvard Yard and watched as their second son, Daniel, in black gown and cap, strode across the stage with his bachelor's degree in one hand. He was bound for business school, destined it seemed for the kind of success his father had achieved. And this thought pleased Max greatly as he sat there with an arm around his wife's shoulders, thinking back through the difficult years that had led to that crowning moment.

A week later, Daniel moved back into the house for the summer. The following Sunday Max took him out for breakfast, and when they returned to the house brought Daniel into his study and spread out a pile of financial statements across his desk. This was a ritual Max performed every three months, and now, for the first time, he included his son in the process.

When he and Daniel finished their review, and Max outlined his plans for rebalancing the portfolio, he asked his son what he thought. Daniel surprised him by pointing out a few inconsistencies in his father's plan, and recommending a few small changes. Far from offended, Max sat back in his chair, grinning broadly. For the first time in his working life he felt he could take a deep breath, secure in the knowledge that should he ever be unable to continue his stewardship of the family fortune, it would be in good hands.

Max and Barbara's oldest son, Jonathan, had followed a different path. He too had graduated from college, but he wasn't a serious student, and had no interest in business. Max had put pressure on him at first to continue his studies, thinking he'd come around eventually, but Barbara, who had raised him, knew better, and convinced her husband to let their eldest son find his own way. He had traveled the world for a year or two after he graduated from college, and had then come back to marry his high school girlfriend. He worked for a small nonprofit housing agency, and seemed content with his life, especially once he heard his wife was pregnant with their first child. As proud as Max and Barbara were of Daniel, his degree and his prospects paled in comparison to the impending addition to the family, living proof that it would endure.

The following Monday morning Max had his annual checkup at the oncologist's, and once that task had been completed he returned home to pack his bags. An old friend of his had just bought a schooner, and Max was going to join the crew on the boat's maiden voyage to the Bahamas. The weather report looked good, although there was a hurricane gathering in the southern Atlantic, and so they charted a coastal route, instead of striking out into deeper water. This meant they'd miss Bermuda, which Max had always wanted to visit, but a long sail inevitably included changes in course, and no one onboard was interested in challenging the Atlantic.

Five days after the schooner left Point Lookout, Long Island, Daniel was sitting at his father's desk when the phone rang. It was the owner of the schooner, a man Daniel had known his whole life. The connection was so bad that it was hard to understand him, but when he finally did it was all he could do to keep the phone in his hand.

Max had disappeared the night before, during his turn at the helm, and although the Coast Guard had mounted a search there was almost no chance he'd be found. Blinking back tears Daniel asked how it had happened, but no one really knew. Max had taken the helm at 2:00 a.m. in choppy seas, and about an hour later all hands had scrambled on deck as the boat began to be broadsided by the waves. The mainsail was untethered, and the boom was swinging back and forth in the wind. By the time they'd made the boat shipshape they realized Max was gone, and so they immediately brought the bow around and headed back the way they'd come. There were clouds covering the moon, though, and the chances of picking anyone out between the swells in the dark of night were small, so they radioed for help and began to circle the area. No trace of him was ever found.

About a week after his father's funeral, Daniel sat down behind his father's desk again, this time with the same documents in front of him that he and his father had reviewed a few weeks earlier. Around noon the phone rang. It was the oncologist's office, calling to confirm that Max would start his chemotherapy the following day.

"His what?" Daniel asked, after identifying himself as Max's son.

"His chemotherapy. You mean he didn't tell you?"

"Didn't tell me what?"

The nurse asked Daniel to hold for just a moment, and a minute later the oncologist came on the line. Max's most recent checkup had revealed tumors throughout his entire body. They didn't know whether it was the same cancer, or something new, and they'd probably never know, but Max needed to begin treatment immediately. If he hadn't spoken to his son about it, surely he'd told his wife?

Daniel thumbed the phone off a few minutes later, having filled the oncologist in on what had happened. Blinking back tears, he tried to focus on the documents in front of him. He couldn't think of a single good reason to tell anyone about the call, least of all his mother. There was only one thing he could do, and that was what his father had taught him to do. So he took a deep breath, opened his father's battered old phone book, and called the three men his father trusted most—his accountant, his lawyer, and his long-time financial advisor.

Years earlier, when his father first began to include him in discussions regarding the family's finances, he had been surprised to hear that his father used a financial advisor. Didn't he know all about investing himself? Wasn't that what he did for a living? His father shook his head. He was a senior executive at an investment firm, and while he supervised those who managed money for the firm's clients, he did not do that work himself. Therefore, he turned to someone he trusted—someone who did that work full time, and had a great track record. Of course he worked closely with his financial advisor—continually monitoring the returns of his investments, and reevaluating his goals—but he had never considered doing the day-to-day transactional work himself, any more than he would have considered acting as his own accountant, or his own lawyer.

Other memories, brought back by the task at hand, continued to distract Daniel as he attempted to work his way through the spreadsheets on his father's desk. His heart wasn't in it, but he knew he had to be well prepared for the meeting he'd set up with his father's trusted advisors for the following week. Just about the time he settled into the job, the office door burst open and his mother came in, a phone in one hand.

"Daniel . . . Jonathan just called from the hospital. Rachel had the baby a week early. It's a boy."

"Is everyone all right?" he asked, getting up from his father's chair.

"Yes, they're fine . . . they're both fine."

"Did they say what they're going to name him?"

His mother blinked, her eyes filling with tears.

"Yes, they did. Jonathan said they're going to name him after your father."

She then rushed out of the room again, anxious to pass the good news along to the rest of the family, and alone once more, Daniel sat down, took a deep breath, and picked up where he'd left off. In spite of the one meeting he'd had with his father shortly before he died, he had not immediately grasped the true extent of his family's wealth.

Five years later, on the anniversary of Max's disappearance, the entire family gathered to dedicate a new wing to the hospital where Max had been treated so many years before. After conferring with his mother and his brother, they all agreed that a new hospital wing, with Max's name on it, would be the most fitting tribute to a man who had not only survived cancer, but had then made the most of each day given to him.

It was a bright, beautiful day, and the sky was suffused with a transcendent light. Leaving his family seated behind him, Daniel walked up to the microphone, and with tears in his eyes read the dedication, which ended with these words:

> . . . and who will be remembered as a man who was not afraid to take reasonable risks to achieve what he wanted in life.

INDEX